Fantasy Art

Learn How to Draw Amazing Fantasy Girls

By Jong Mac

Table of Contents

Disclaimer

While all attempts have been made to verify the information provided in this book, the author does assume any responsibility for errors, omissions, or contrary interpretations of the subject matter contained within. The information provided in this book is for educational and entertainment purposes only. The reader is responsible for his or her own actions and the author does not accept any responsibilities for any liabilities or damages, real or perceived, resulting from the use of this information.

The trademarks that are used are without any consent, and the publication of the trademark is without permission or backing by the trademark owner. All trademarks and brands within this book are for clarifying purposes only and are the owned by the owners themselves, not affiliated with this document.

Introduction

Fantasy creatures have been a part of our world for a long time. Fairies, elves, angels and similar creatures may not be real; but they play an important role in the culture in our movies and literature. Their origin is an ancient one; but they still continue to play a role in our society, whether it be stories like Peter Pan or movies such as The Lord of the Rings or the Harry Potter movies. Some of the common fantasy creatures that are included in this book are fairies, angels, and female characters that are part animal and part human.

Fairies are fictional creatures that are European in origin. When most people think of fairies, they think of magical tiny beings that have wings and large ears. Also, they are believed to have magical powers. The word, fairy comes from the old French word, 'faerie', which means enchantment. In Europe, the word, fairy is often equated with lots of magical beings including goblins and sprites. It seems to be the English that equate the word with the fairies we most commonly think of- a tiny being that flies, has magical powers and is often depicted as female. The first depiction of fairies in English literature date back to the thirteenth century.

They were popular in the world of medieval romances such as Edmund Spenser's *The Fairie Queen*. In writings of the fifteenth century, King Arthur was taken to Avalon to the land of the fairies when he died. Later, Shakespeare himself included the subject in his works such as *A Midnight Summer's Dream*. In the early 1900's, Peter Pan became a very popular story featuring the most popular fairy in modern times, Tinkerbell. Peter Pan is still very popular and was not only made into a feature film; it has also been made into play productions that are still put on all across the world. Fairies are still very much a part of our culture even to this day.

Angels are thought of as beings that are spiritual intermediaries between heaven and earth. Often they are portrayed as providing guidance for human beings and guardians. The word, angel is derived from the Latin word, angelus, which means, 'messenger'. The Christian idea of an angel is thought to have derived from the Hebrew idea, which may have come from Egyptian ideas. Angels such as Gabriel, Michael, and Raphael all served as messengers between humans and heaven. Angels also feature in the Islamic faith; and they serve the same purpose that they serve in the Jewish and Christian faiths- they are messengers between human beings and God. Angels also feature prominently in the world of art, especially with regards to ancient art. Even in modern films, angels serve as figures of guidance and as messengers.

This book also features a female character that is part cat and part human. This fantasy creature has its origins in the comic book world of Marvell comics. They are thought in the comic world to have been created from ordinary house cats by a sorcerer named Ebrok. Also, the character, Cat Woman is a villain in the world of Bat Man and Robin and was featured in recent Bat Man movies.

Whether it is angels or fairies, we often think of these beings as female. These creatures are often depicted as beautiful, young women that possess motherly qualities. They will continue to captivate us in popular culture with their beauty and power, whether it be in new works of literature or motion pictures. Female characters have grace and kindness that draws us to them due to the fact that female energies are nurturing energies.

Chapter 1 – Fairy Princess

Fairies are creatures that capture the imagination. Children believe in them and adults usually don't; but either way they cast a spell on us with their beauty and magical appearance.

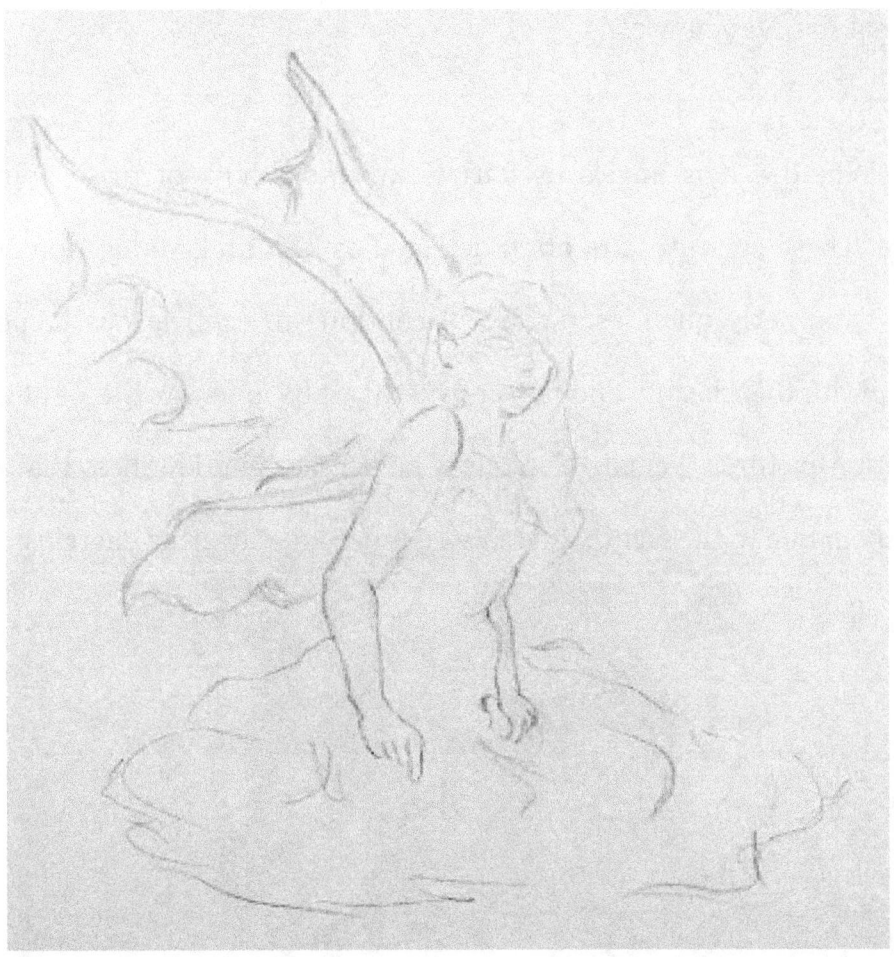

Draw the outline of the figure with light strokes. Make curved wings that come to points on their underside. Sketch long, tube-shaped arms and a ruffled shape to form the dress. Make the outline of her face and hair; and draw the oval-shapes that will become the eyes.

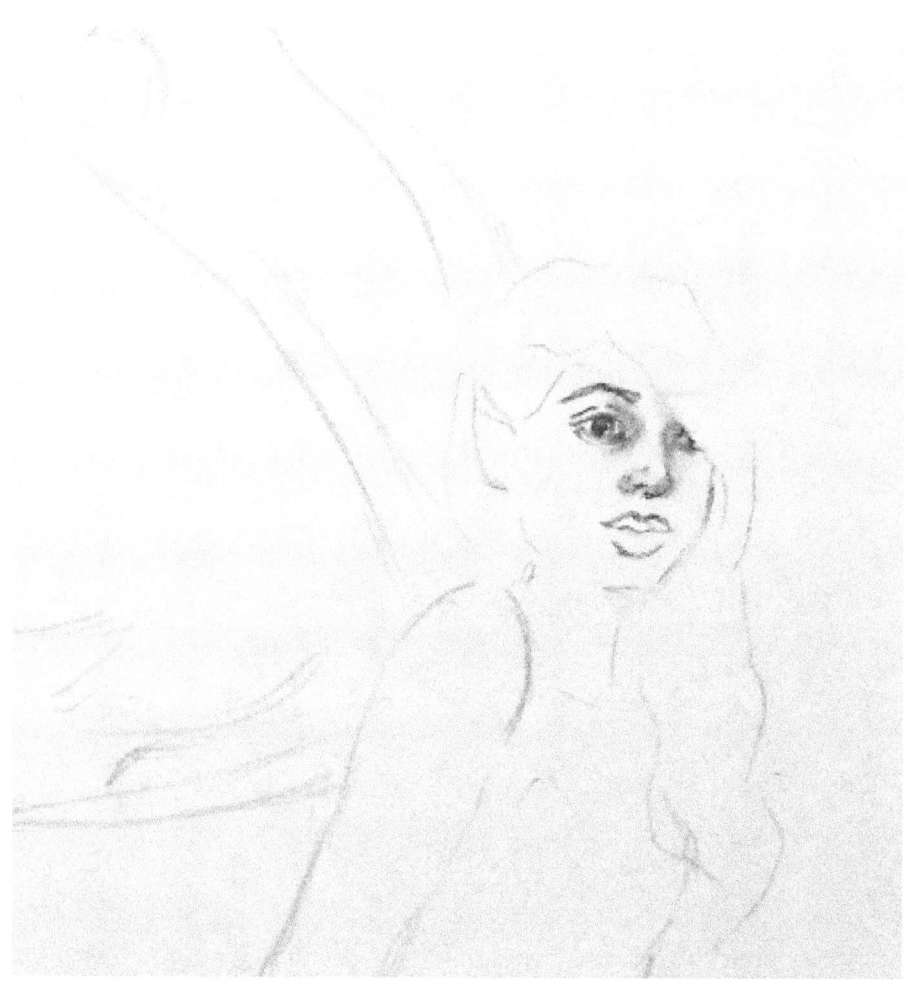

Use very dark shading to make the eyebrows. Inside the oval-shaped eyes, make a dark circle; but leave a couple of spots unshaded. Make some subtle marks around the outside of the eye and shade using the side of the pencil on the left side of the eye. Carefully draw in the curve of the nostril and the nostril itself. Make some shading along the bottom of the nose. Draw the corner of the left eye. Draw in the 'm' shaped top lip, an 'm' shape beneath this for the opening of the mouth; and a 'u' shape for the bottom lip.

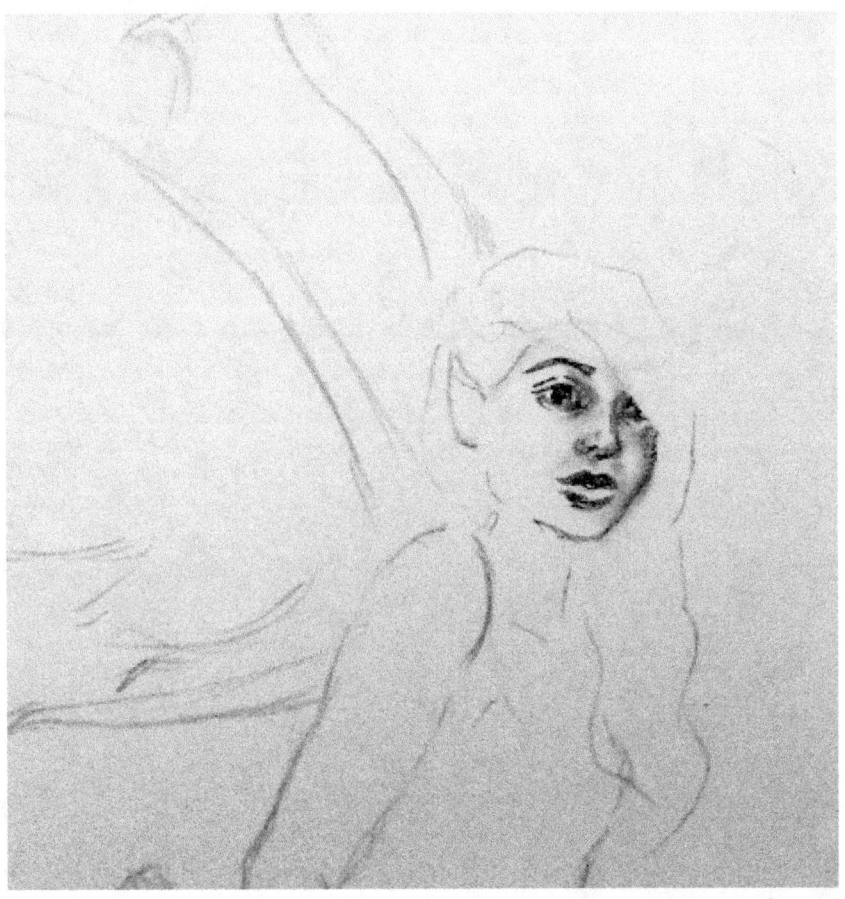

Now, using the side of the pencil make some darker shading around the left side of the right eye, beneath the nose and along the edge of the left cheek.

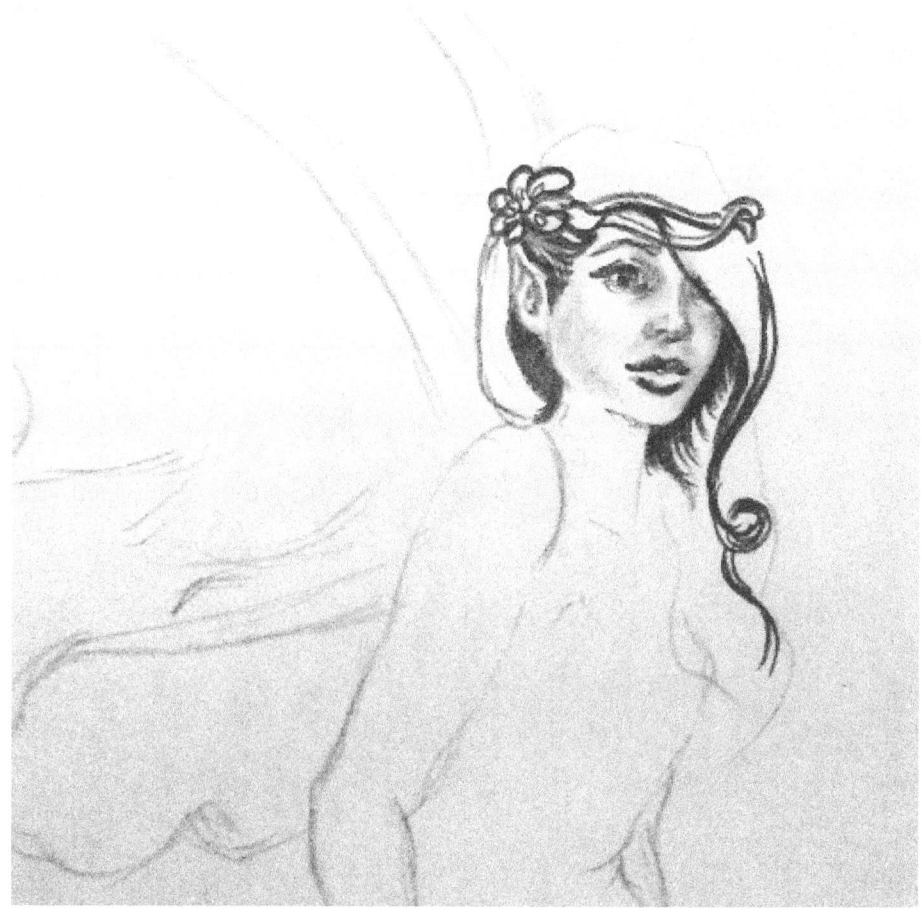

Make very dark oval-shaped flower petals above the ear and place small oval shapes inside of it. Draw long ribbons extending across the forehead of the figure. Make the left edge of her hair come down into a loop. No, add some dark shading on the lower portion of both sides of the face. On the left side, make sure the shading resembles shafts of hair. Add in the detail on the inside of her ear and some subtle shading on the right cheek.

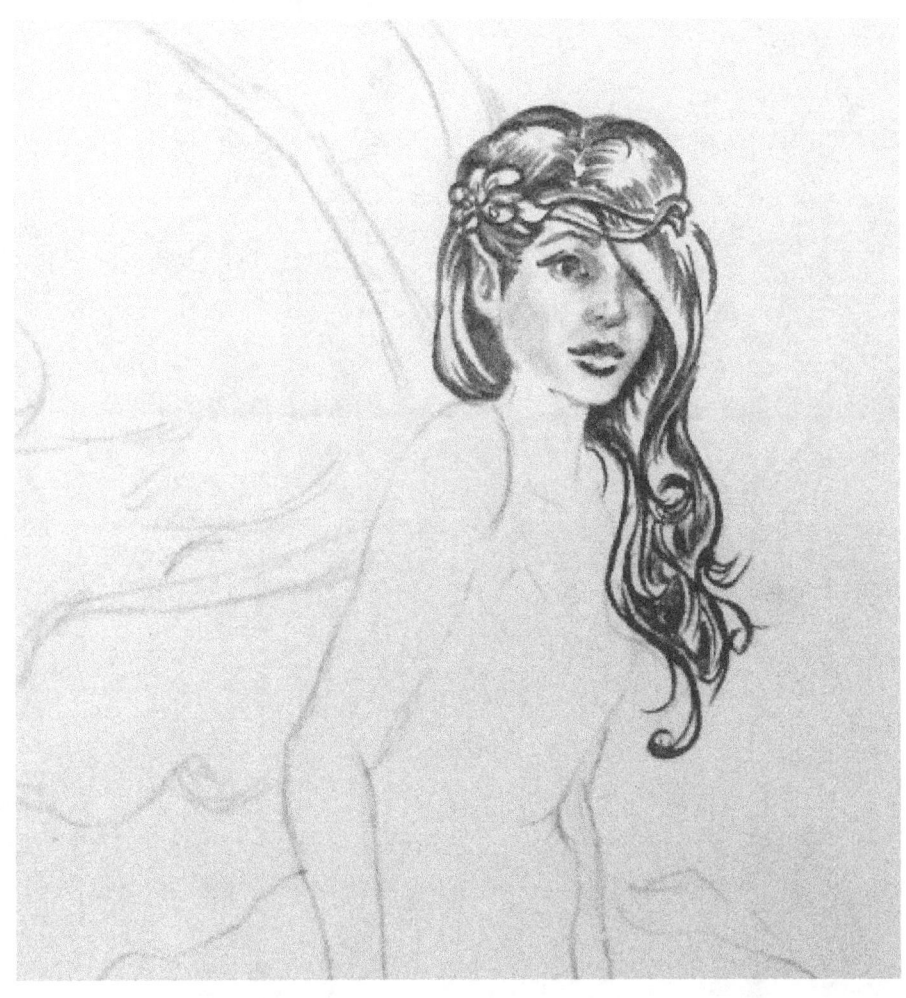

Add in stenciled marks for her hair on the top of her head and in the other areas of her hair indicated in the drawing. Add the loops and strands with areas of dark shading on the lower portion of her hair.

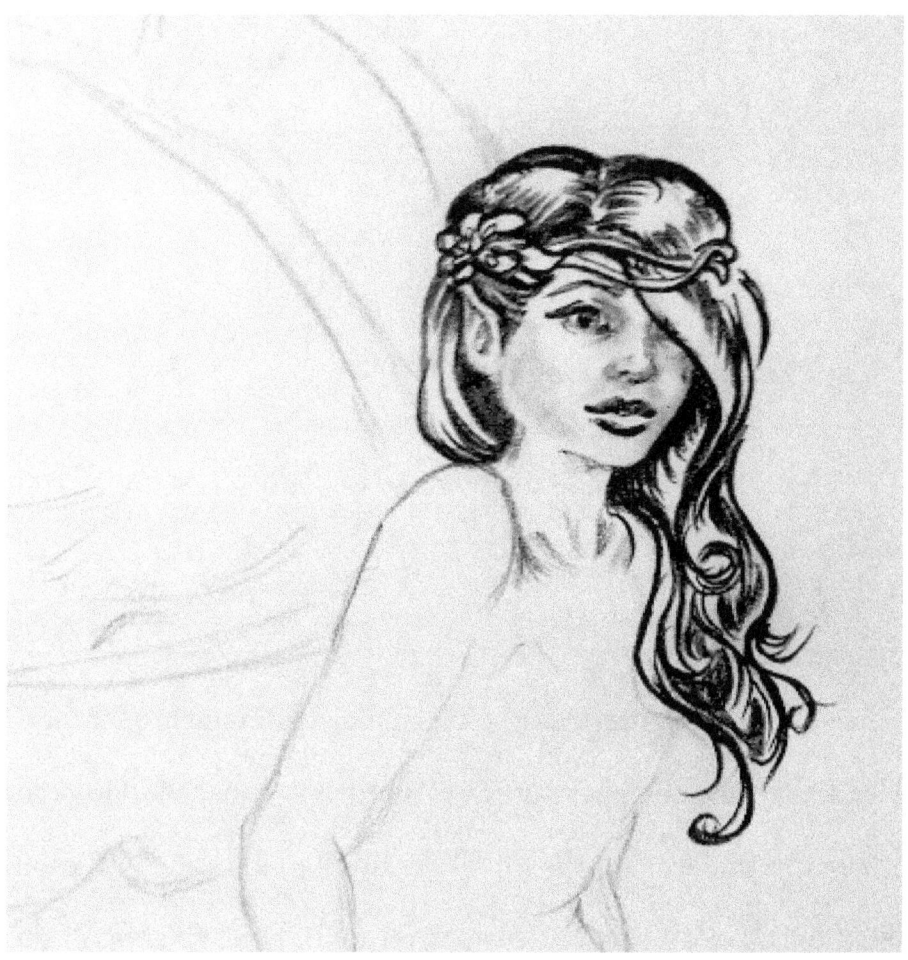

Make some subtle, 'v'-shaped marks around her neck.

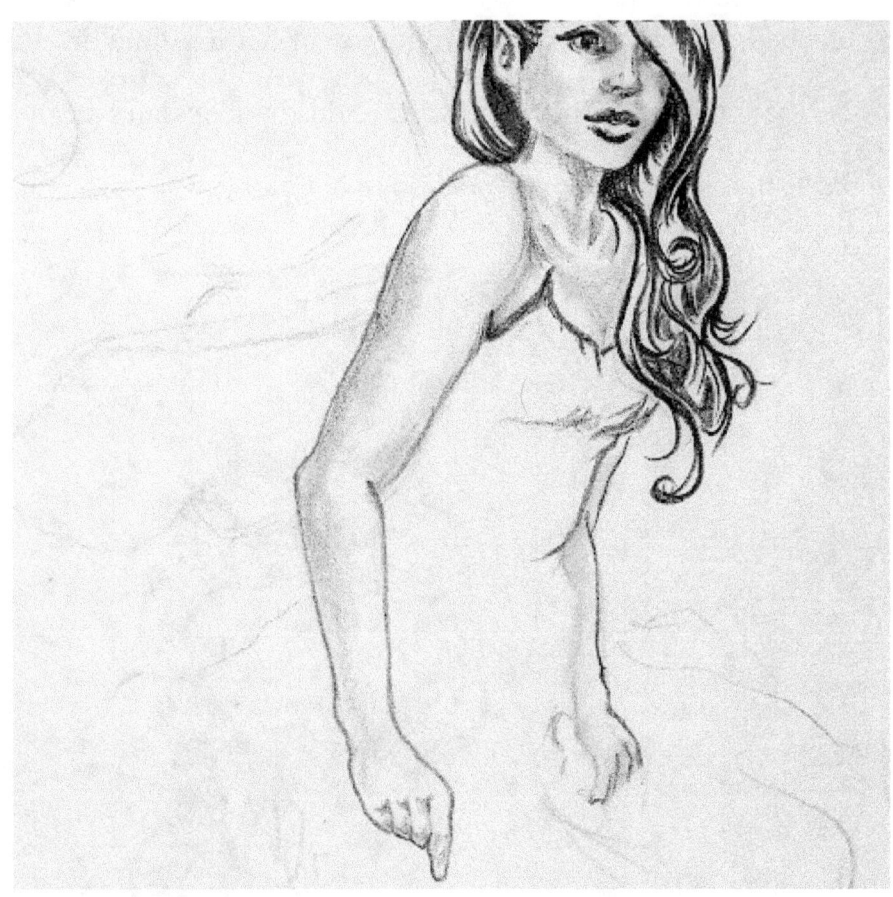

Along the side of her arms, make some subtle shading using the side of the pencil lead. Go over the upper outline of her dress to make it darker and add in subtle marks underneath the top of the dress to indicate her bosom. Add some subtle lines with small 'u' shapes on top for the fingers on the right hand.

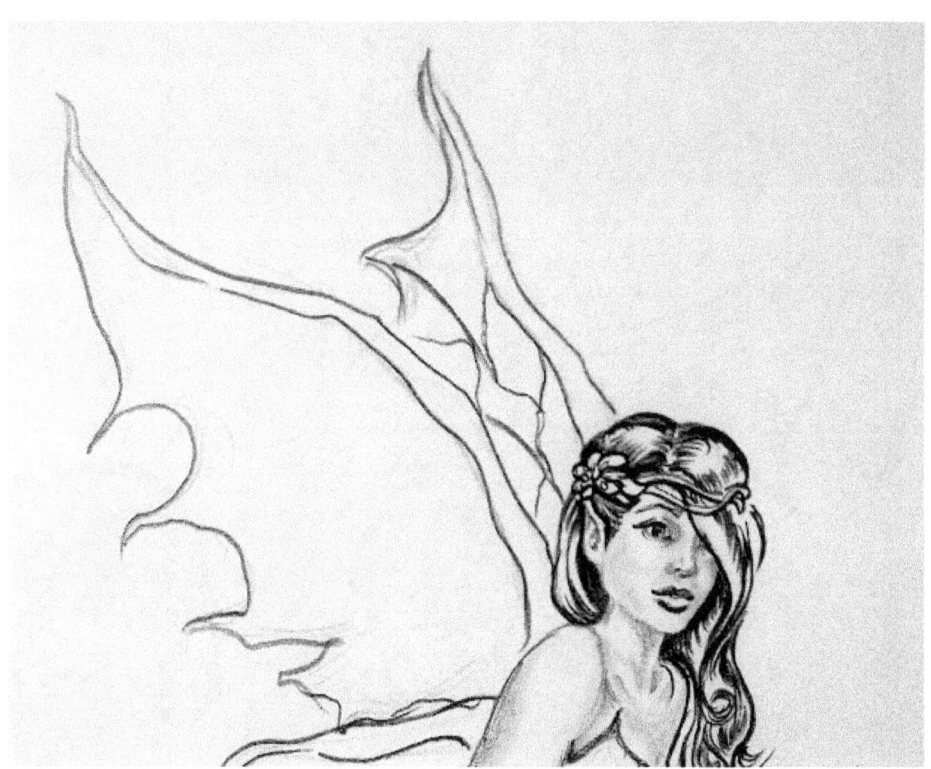

Go over the outline of the wings with darker marks. Add some irregular diamond shapes in between the wings as indicated in the drawing.

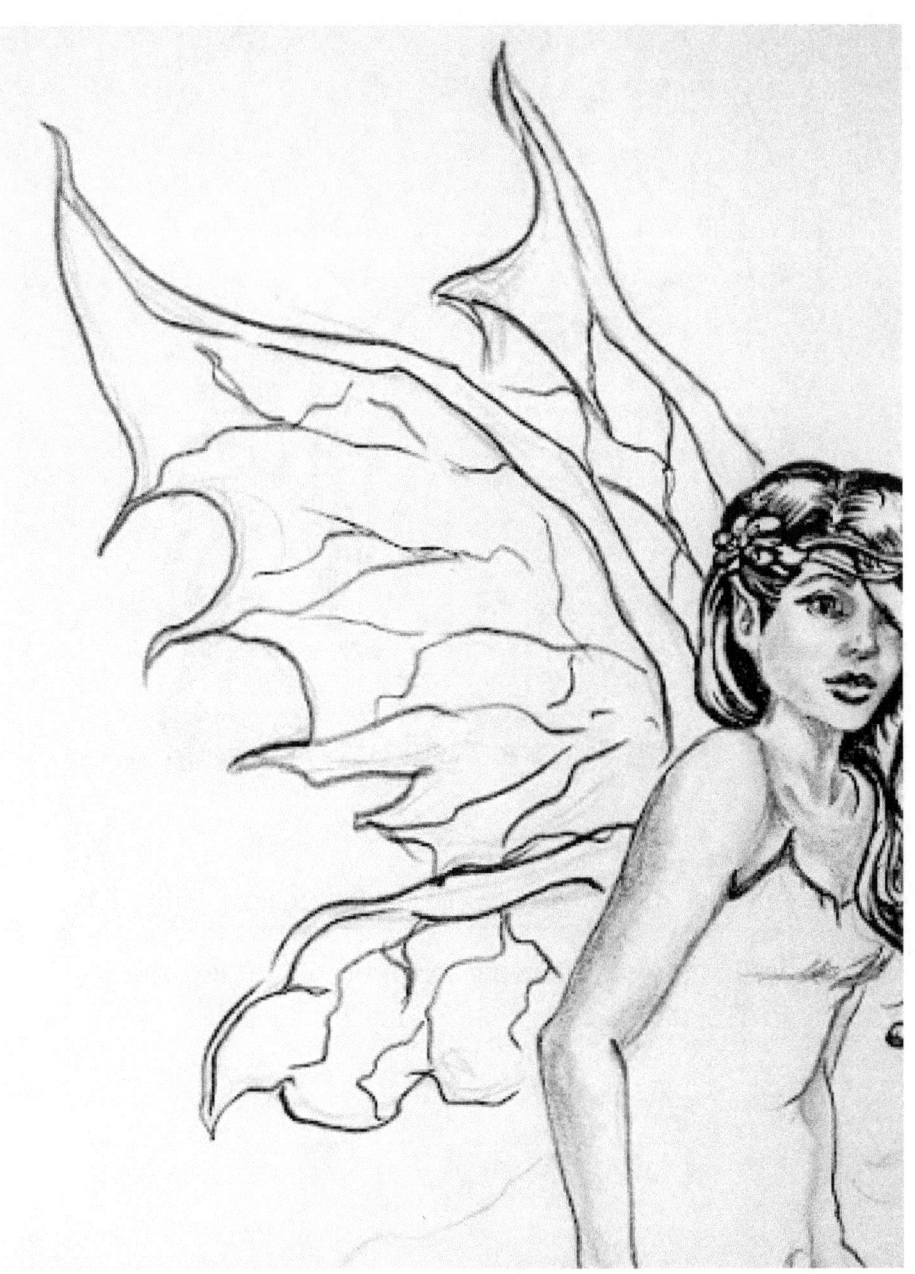

Add some curved, irregular lines inside of the wings as indicated by the drawing.

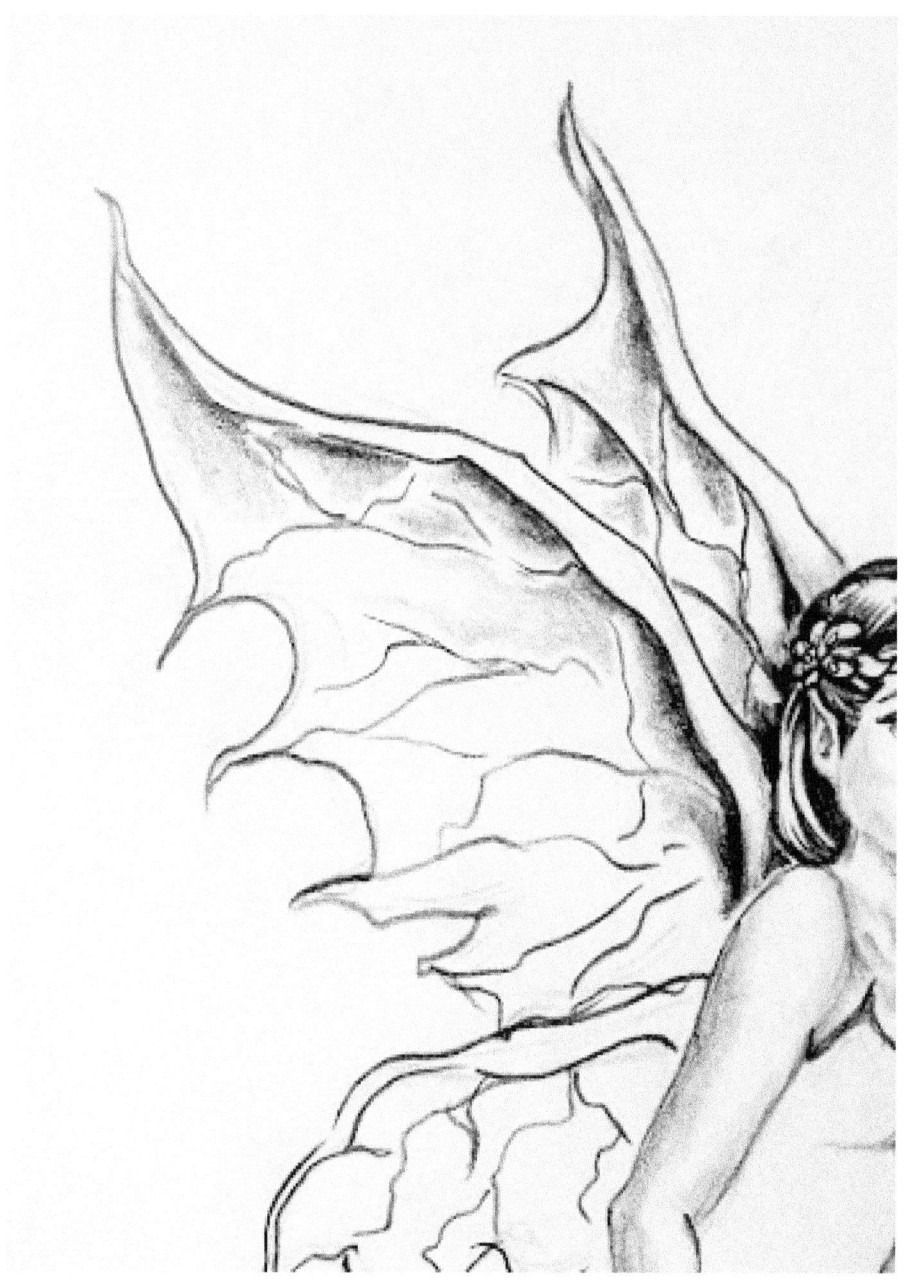

Along the top edge of the wings, make some dark shading that becomes lighter and more subtle as you extend outwards form the edges.

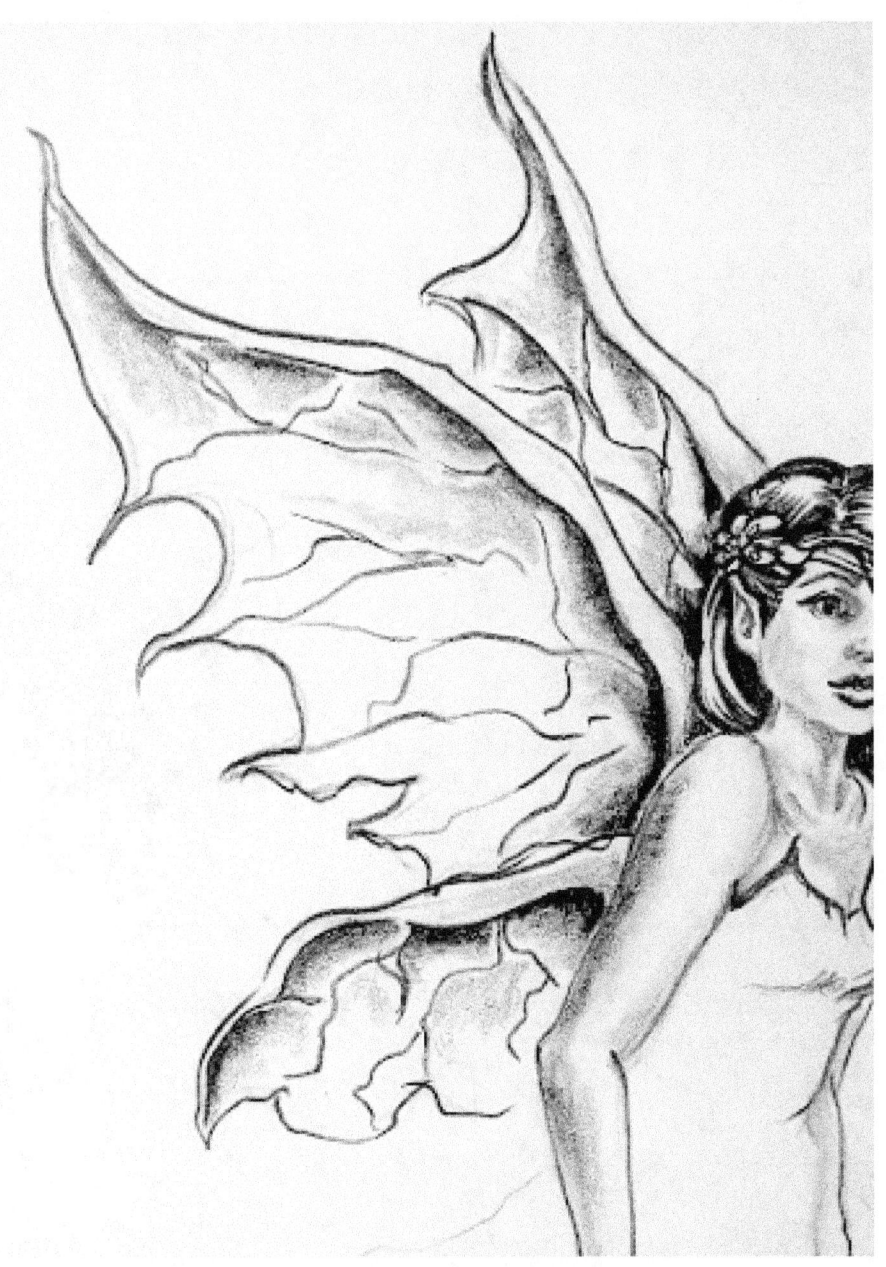

Make some darker shading along the lower portion of the wing that becomes lighter and more subtle as you go extend downwards.

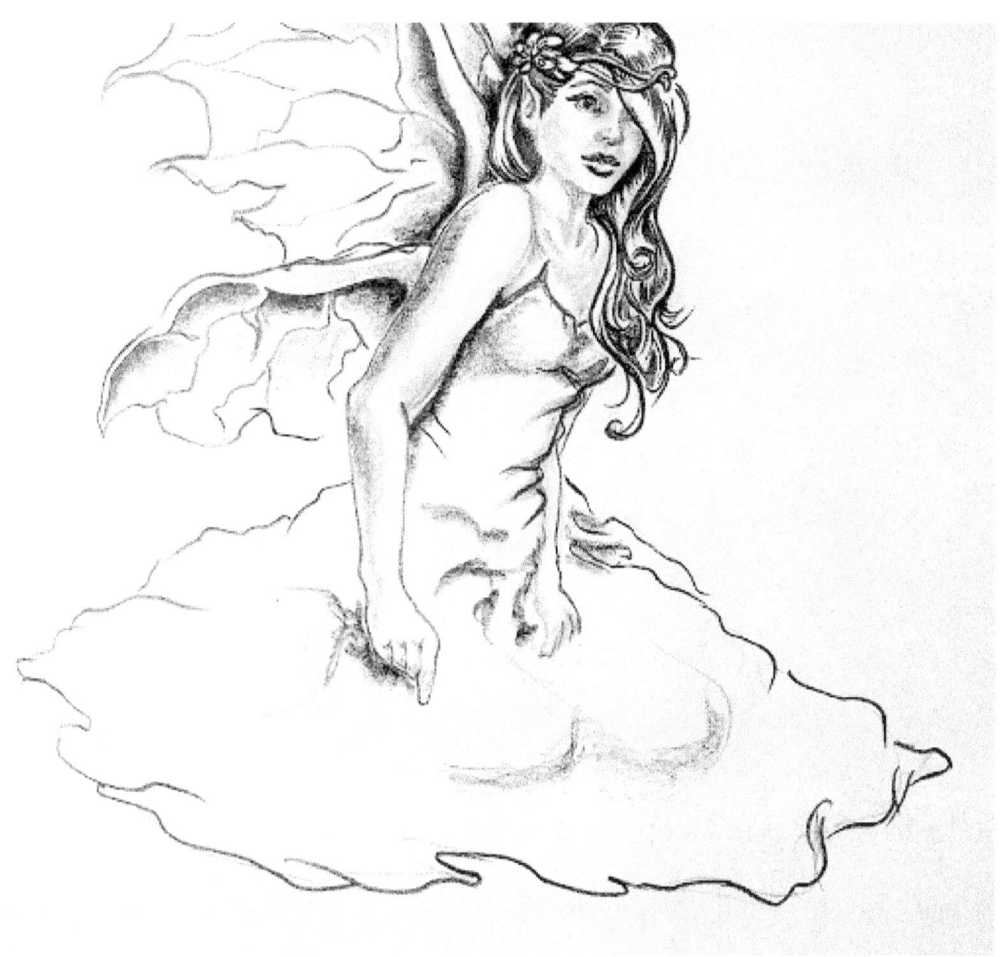

Go over the lower outline of the dress with darker marks. Add some areas of shading to indicate her knees poking through. Add more subtle shading in between and around the hands as indicated in the drawing.

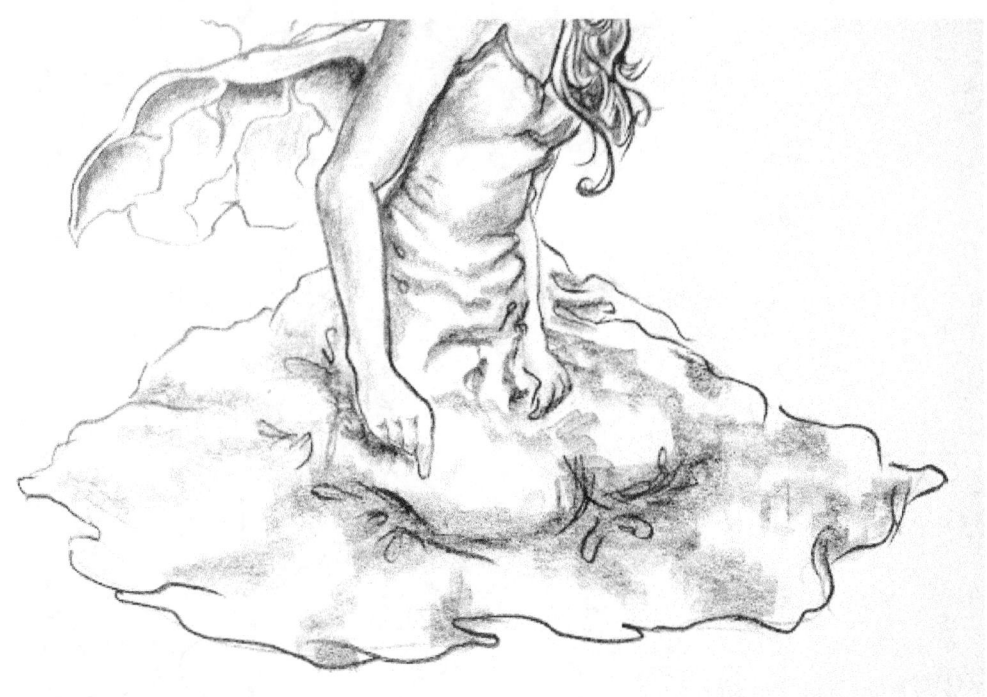

Make irregular dark loops and lines to the right of the right hand and beneath the arms to indicate ruffles in the dress. Add lots of areas of shading all over the dress as indicated.

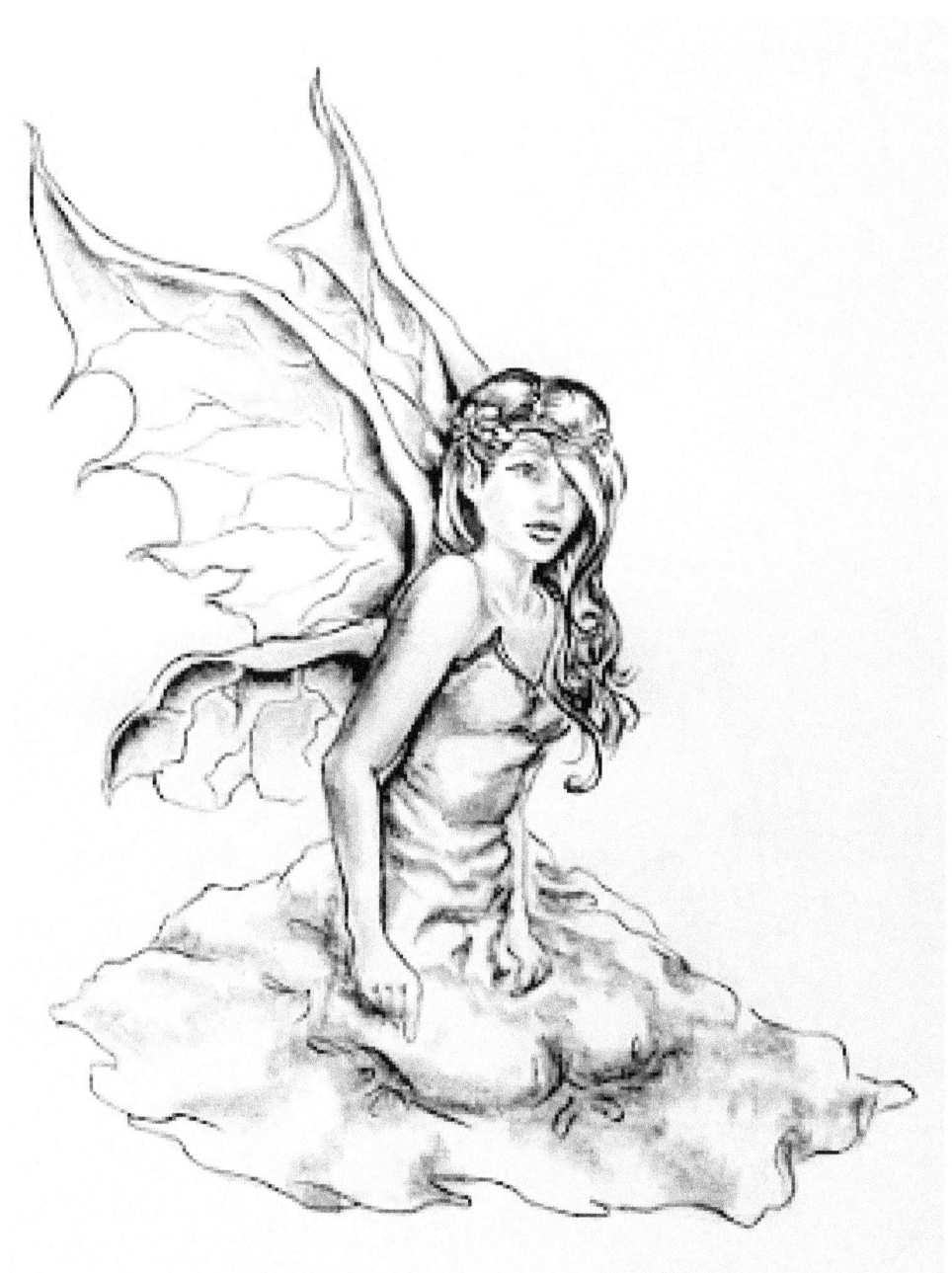

Here is the full view of the fairy princess. Check and see if there are any details you may have left out and draw them in.

Chapter 2 – Angel

This winged fantasy girl is an angel. She has her wings folded as if she has landed after taking flight. You can see the look of kindness on her face. Angels like her are benevolent creatures that serve as guardians and messengers.

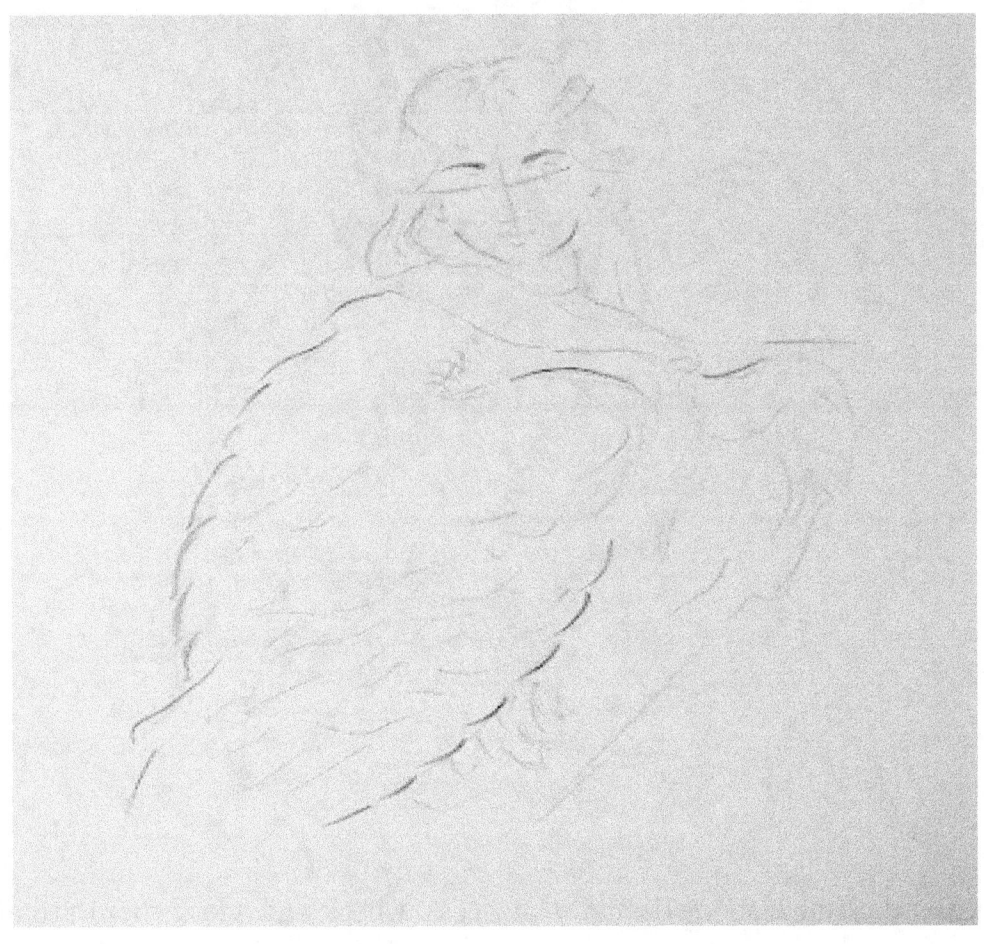

Make the outline of the figure, making curved marks for the wings that don't touch one another. For the face, make a cross-like shape in the center to help with spacing the facial features. Add dark eyebrows above this. Draw the subtle markings on the wings.

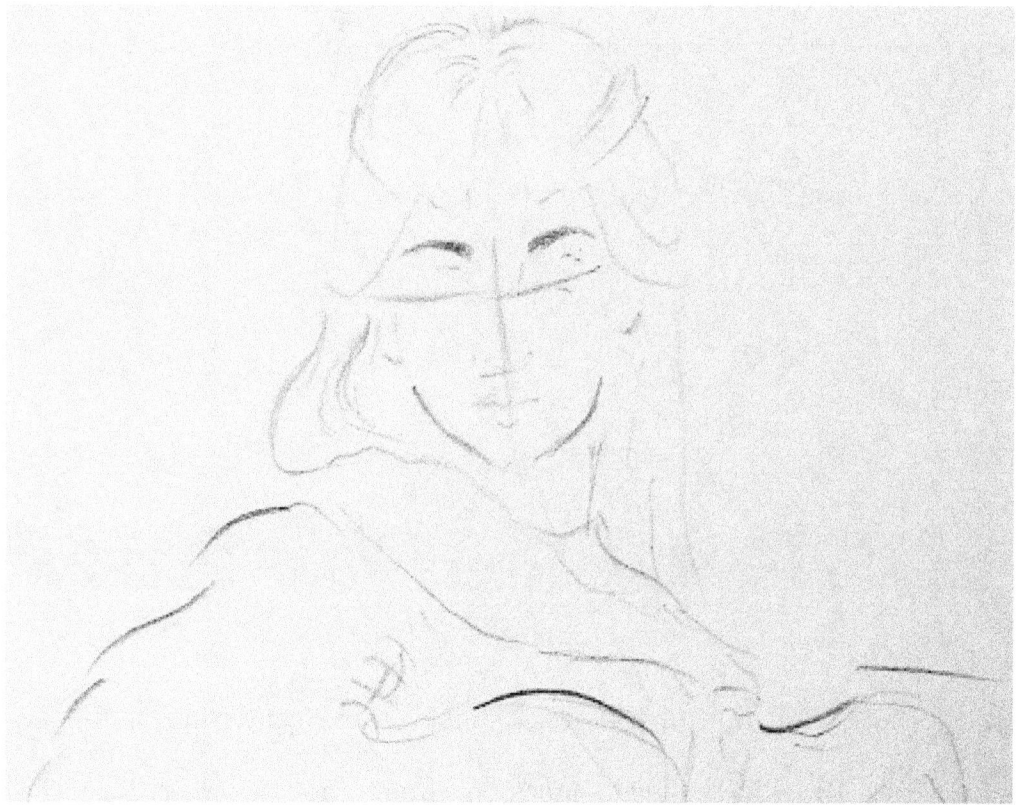

Carefully add in the curved shape of the mouth and nose. Add in subtle curved marks to indicate the parting of her hair and the shape of the crown on the edge of her head. Add subtle markings for the hair.

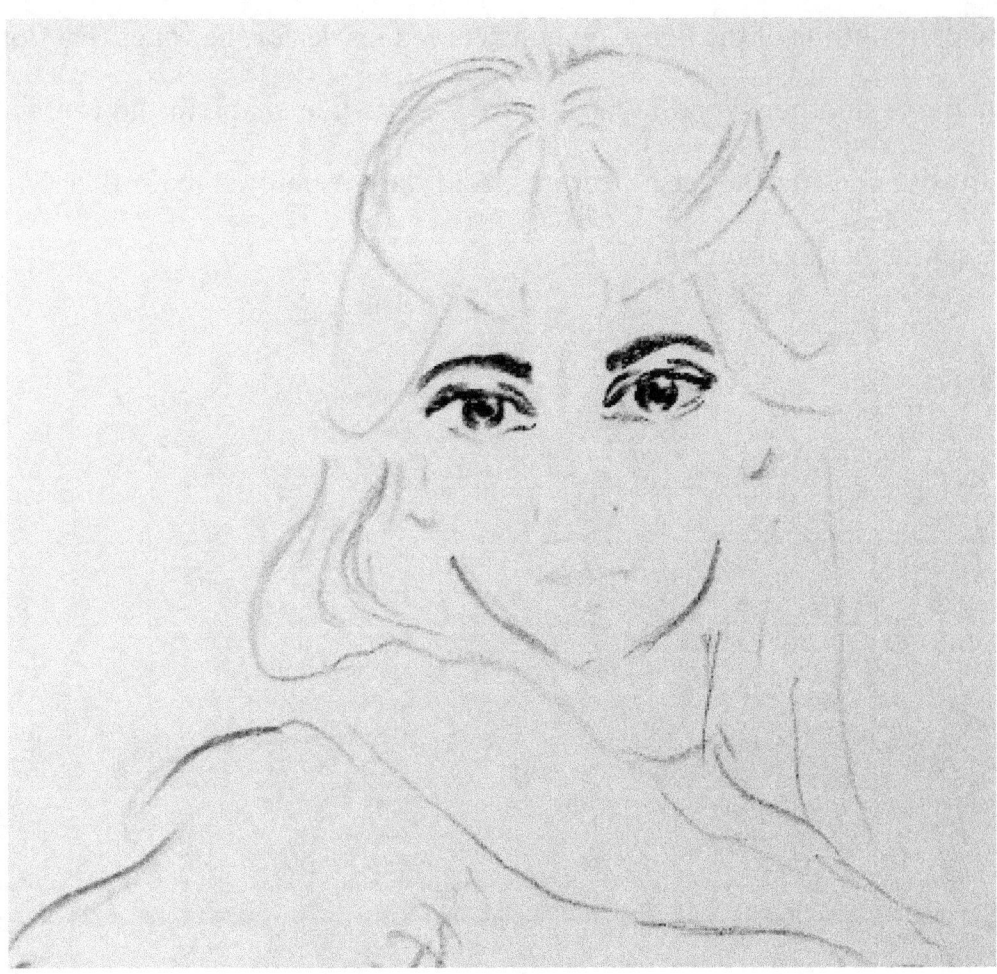

Use the horizontal line of the cross shape as the centerline of the oval-shaped eyes. Draw in the oval shapes and then erase the cross. Now shade the eyebrows heavy and dark. Use dark shading to form the upper portion of the eyes and dark circles for the pupils.

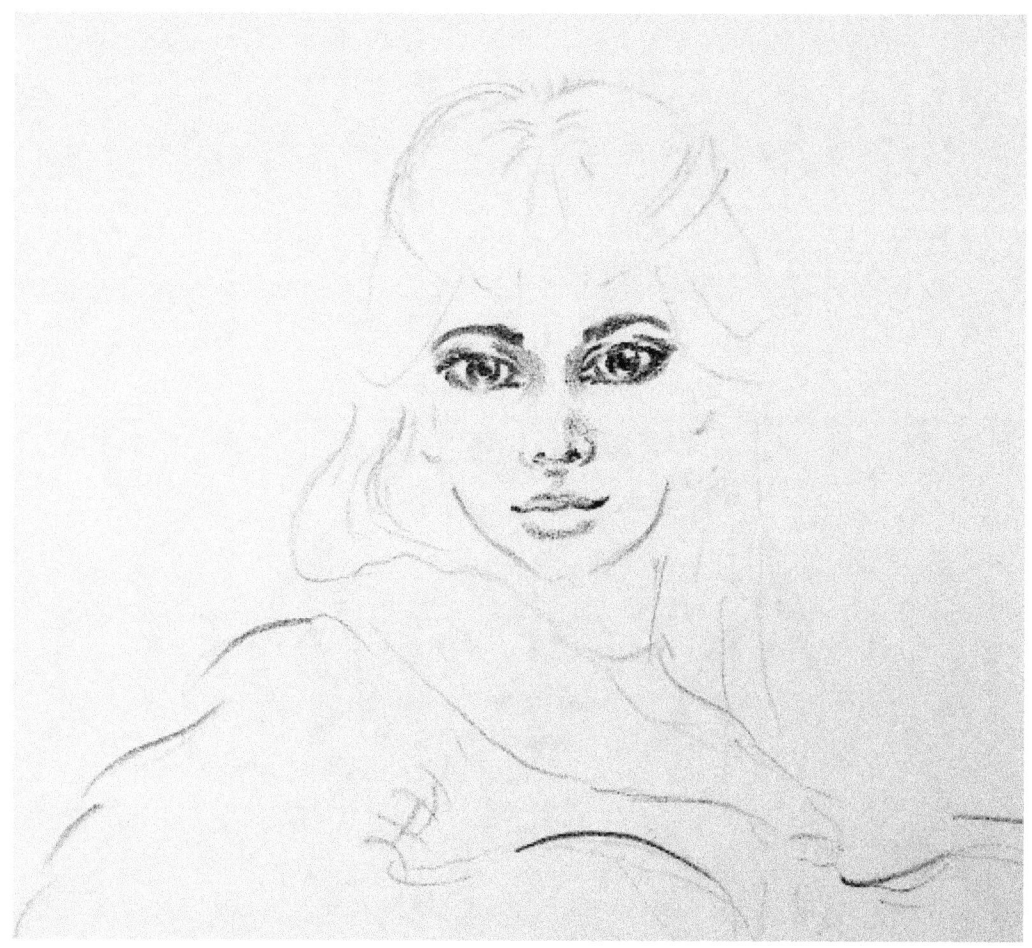

Add some subtle shading on the inside edges of both eyes to indicate the bridge of her nose. Beneath the bridge use subtle curved marks to make the outline of her nose and darker, circular marks for the nostrils. Make a flattened, dark 'm' shaped for the mouth opening and add some shaded lines above and below this for the lips.

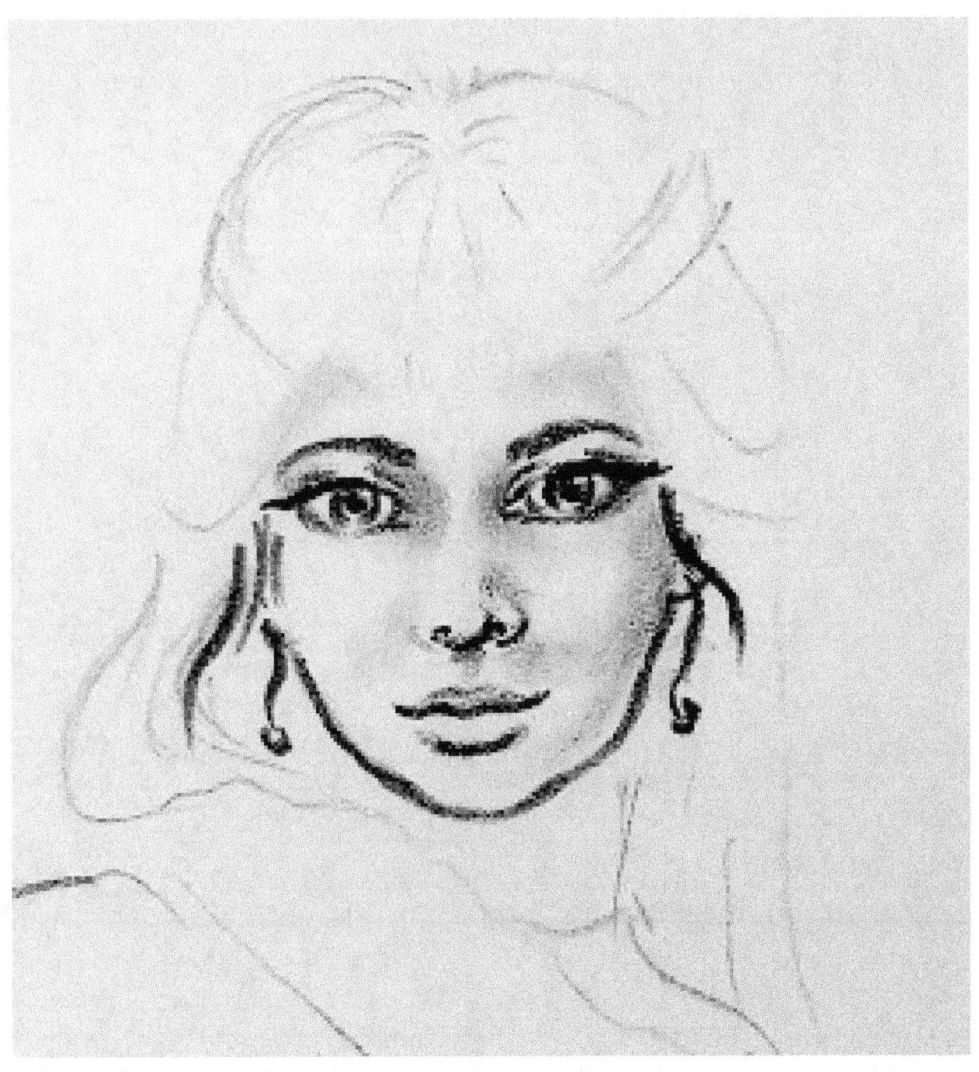

Along the cheeks and above the eyes, do some light shading. Go over the bottom edge of the chin and a few of the hairs on either side of the face with darker markings.

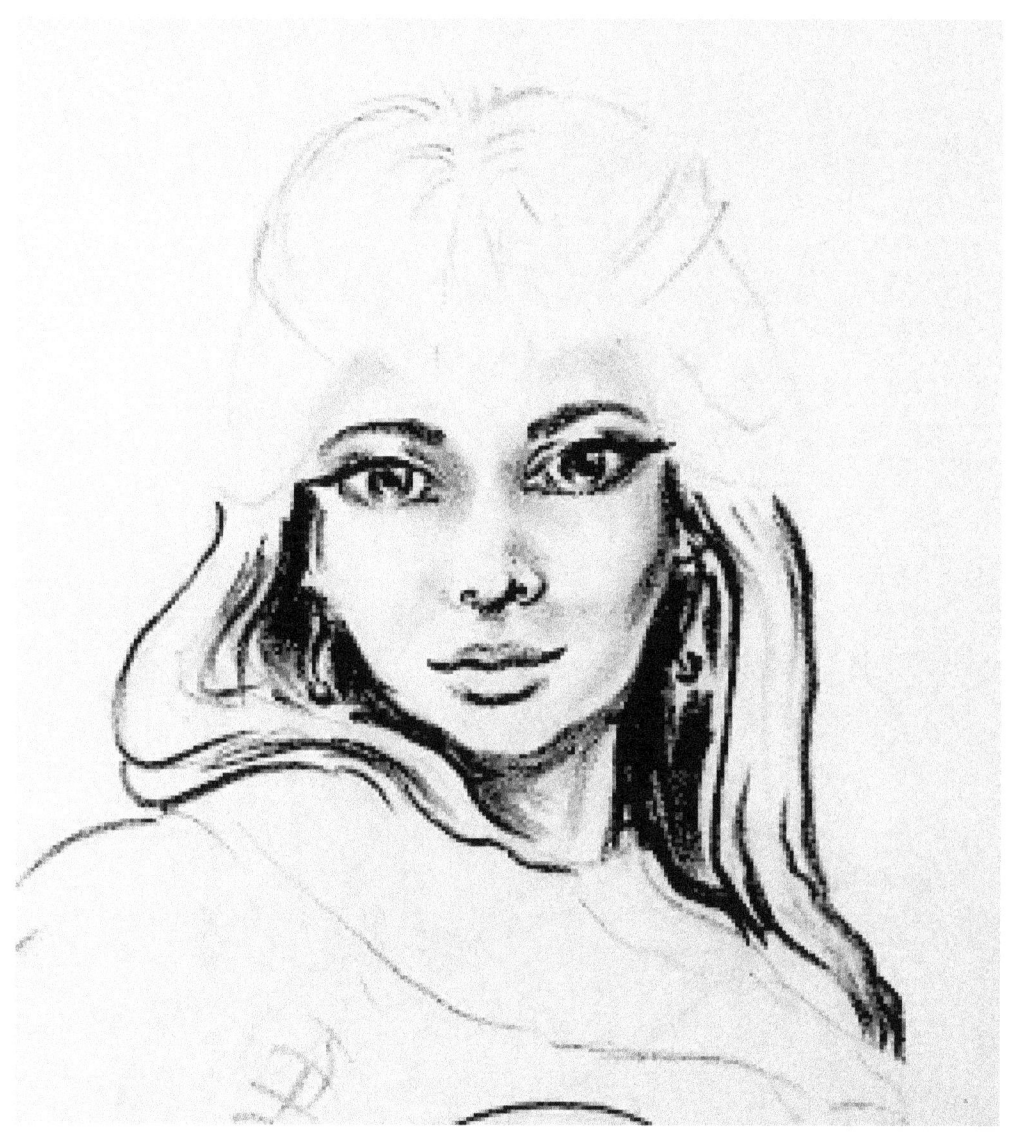

Now go over the outline of her hair with darker markings. Add in the darker regions of shading adjoining the face and the dark, curved marks of her hair.

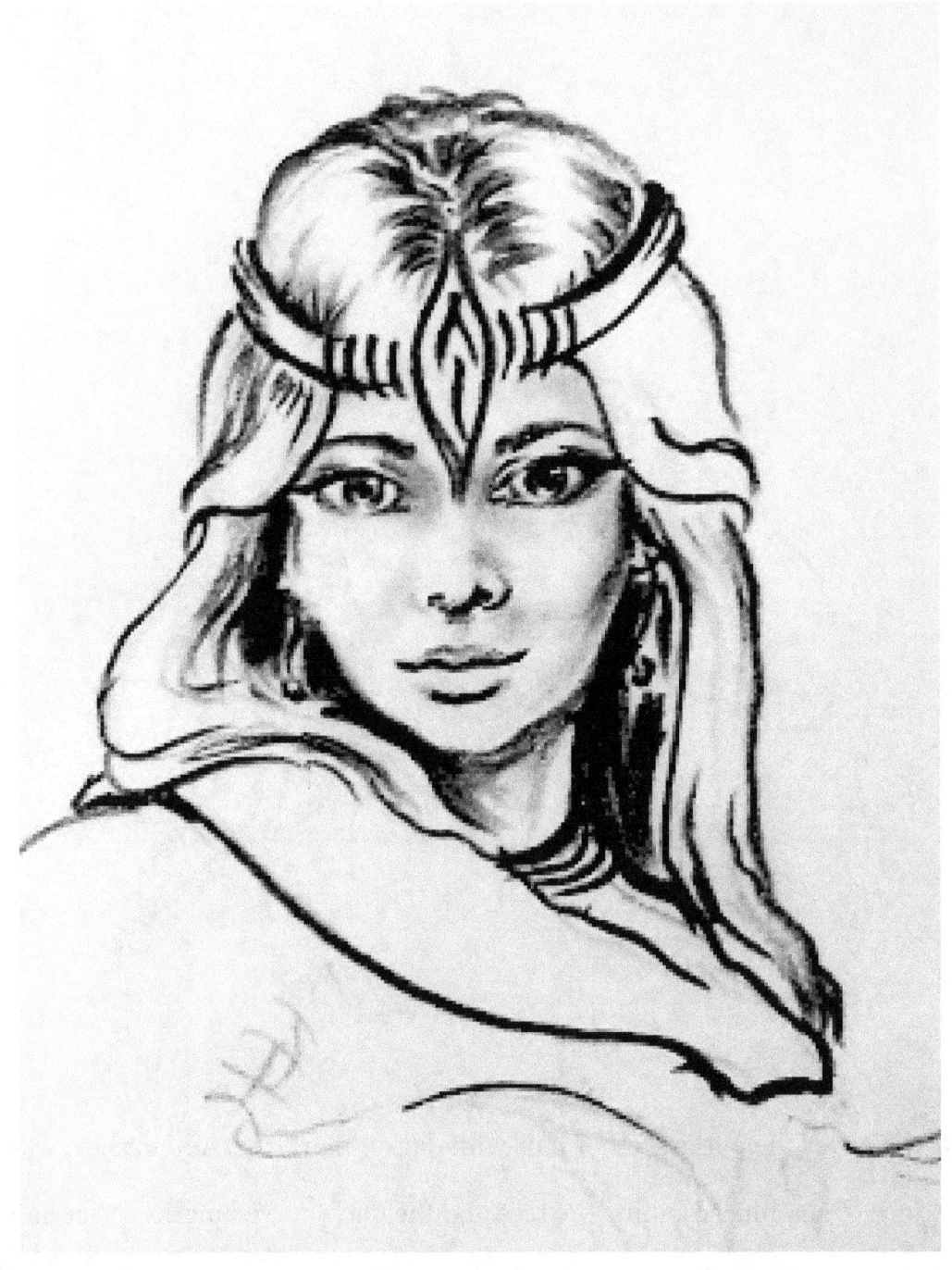

Make the darker markings of her hairline. Draw the curved, rectangular shape of her crown with a pointed oval shape in the center. Add darker marks on the left and right, upper portions of her hair and the top portion of her cape, above the wings.

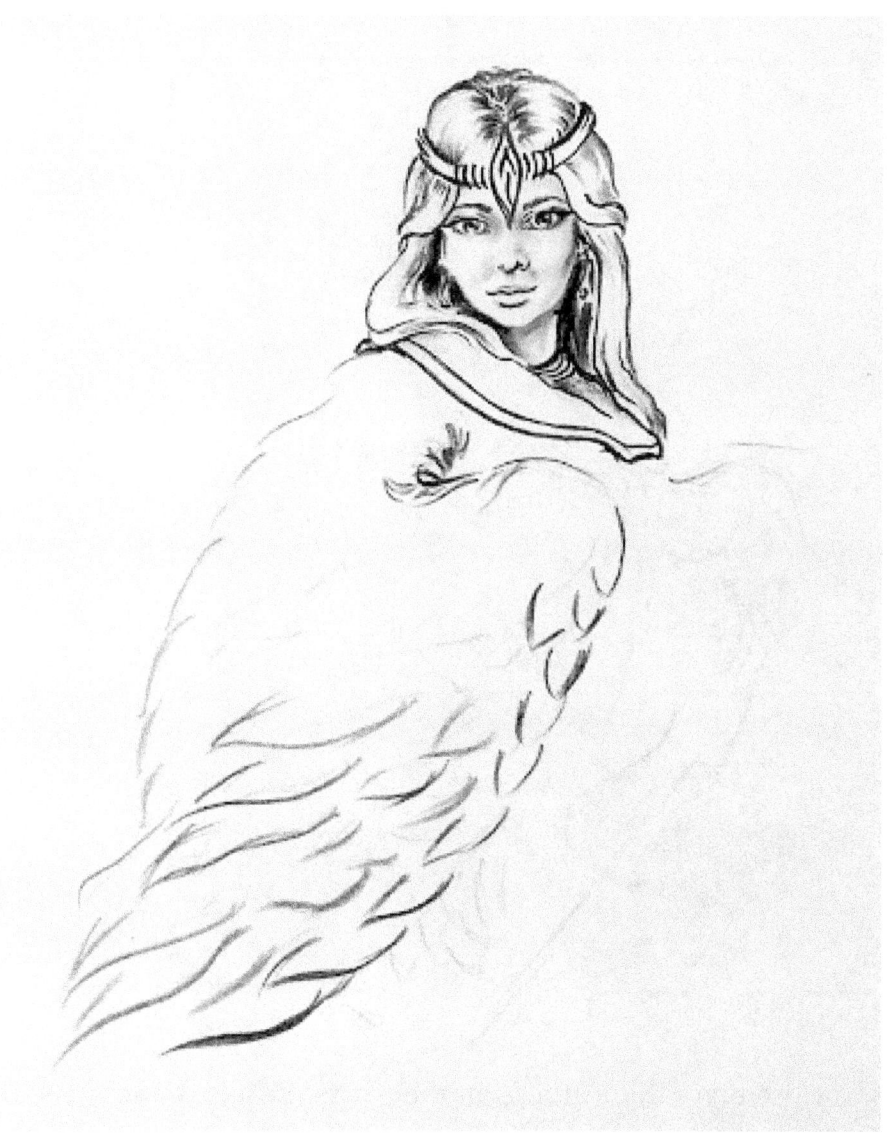

Go over the partial, pointed oval shapes for feathers on her wings. Add a stripe along the edge of her cape below the neck.

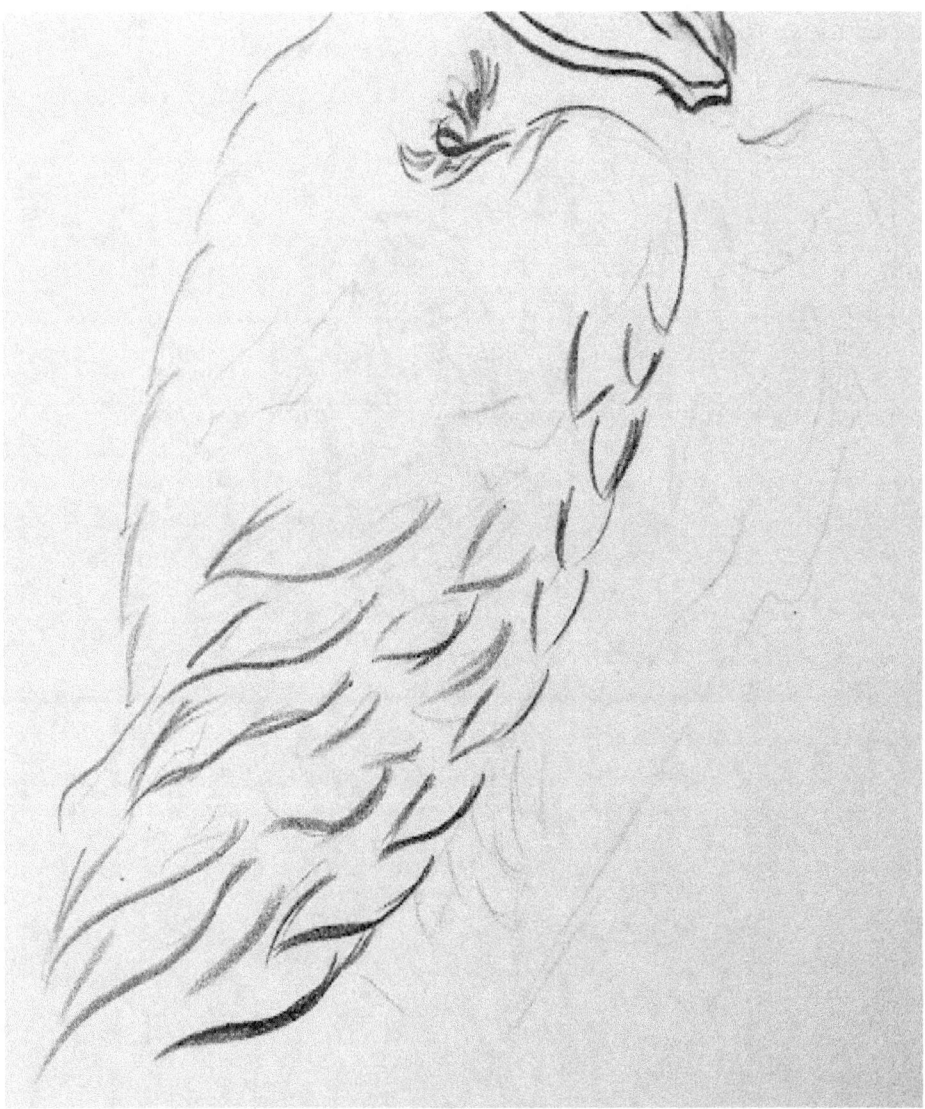

Here is a close up of the feathers on the wings. Be sure to keep the feathers from touching and make the ones on the left side slightly darker.

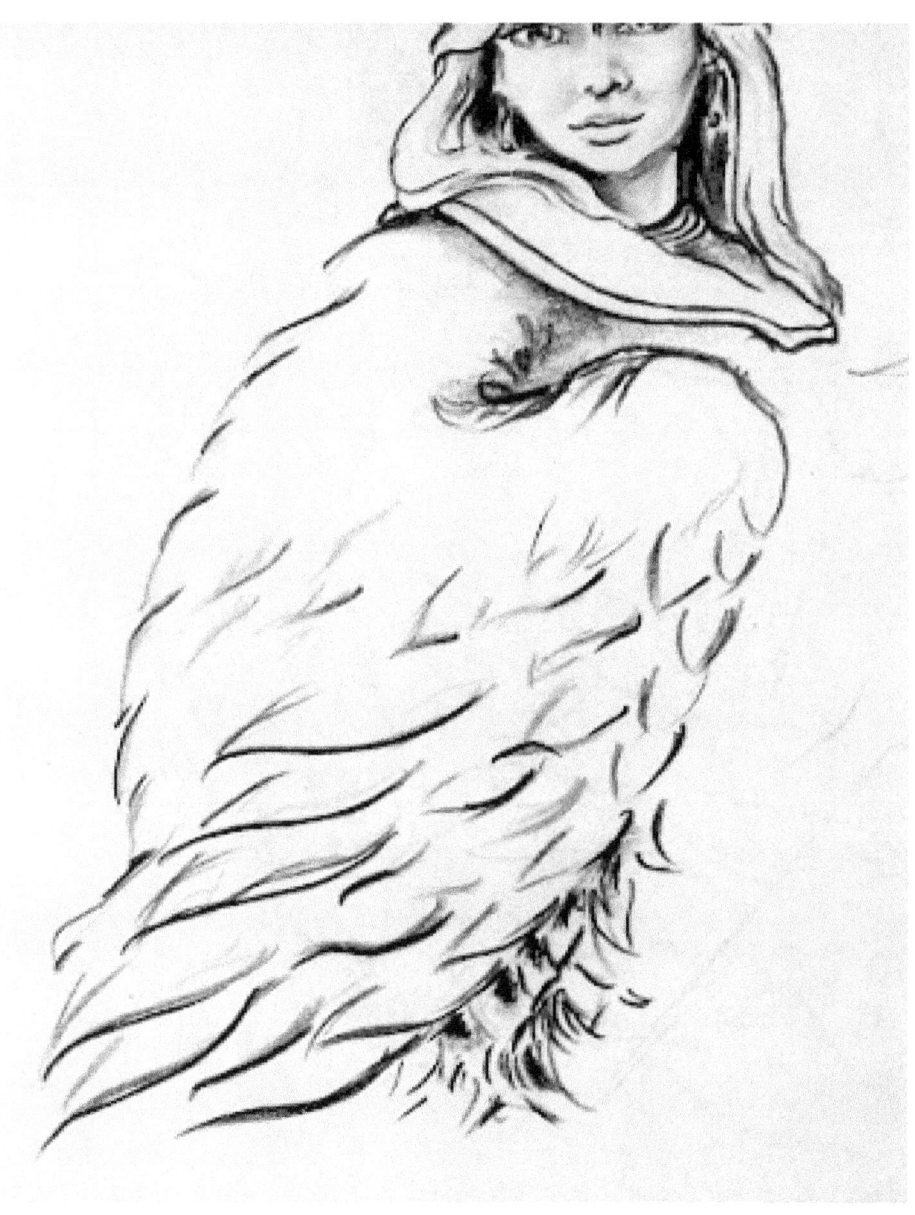

Add in some subtle shading below the stripe you made on the cape. Ass in some curved marks on the lower left potion of the wing and some darker, tornado-like shapes as indicated in the picture.

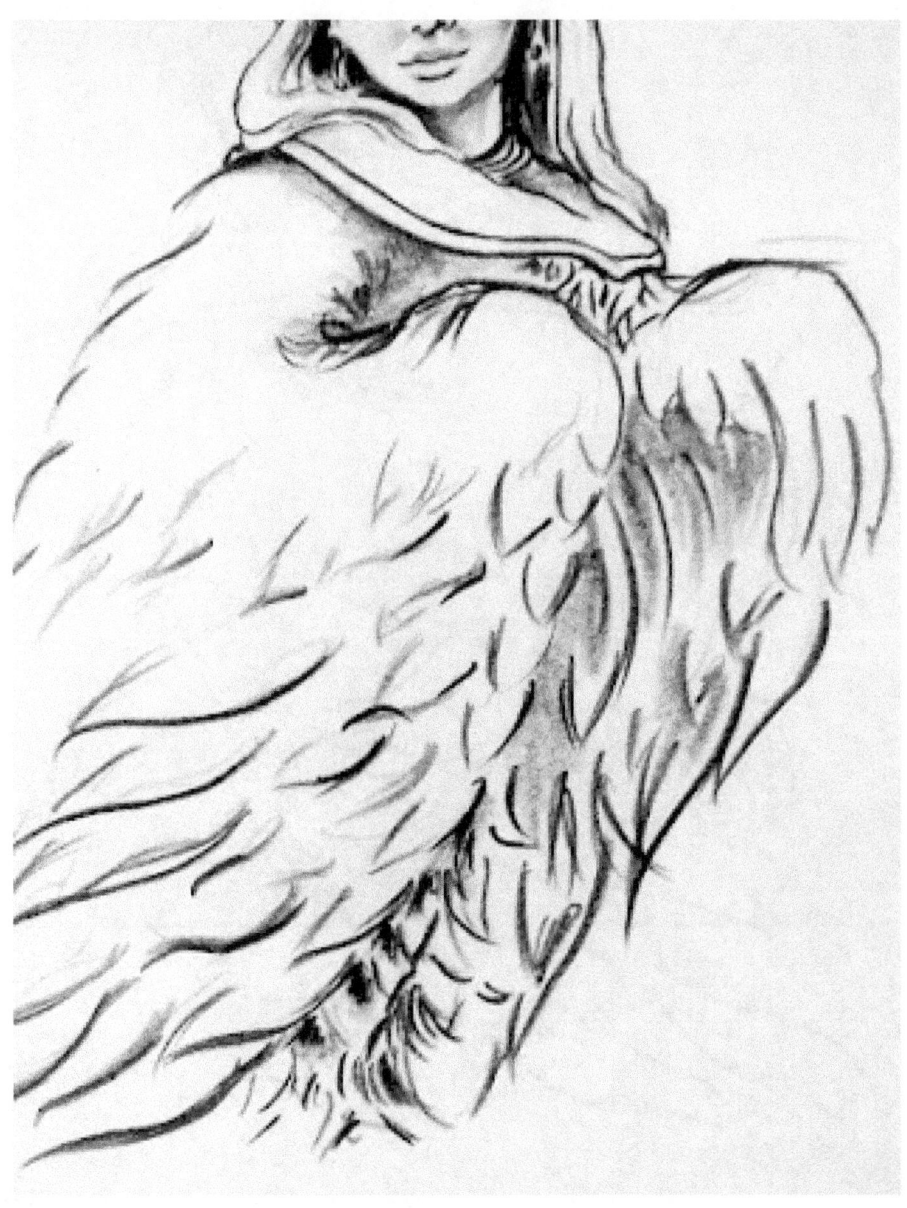

Add in the curved marks that will be the feather on the left wing. Add some shading along the line where the two wings meet extending along the top portion of the left wing.

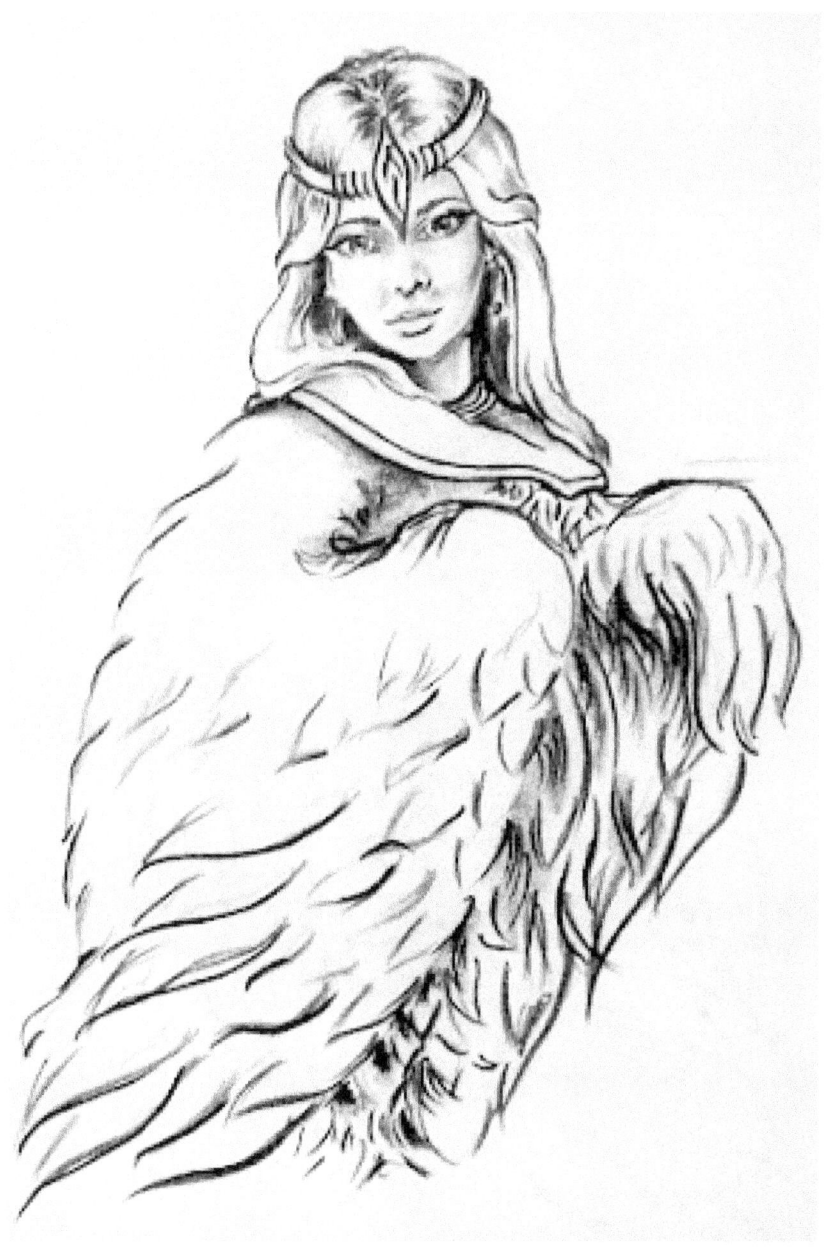

Add some smaller, curved lines beneath the upper portion of the left wing and other areas of the left wing and where the two wings meet.

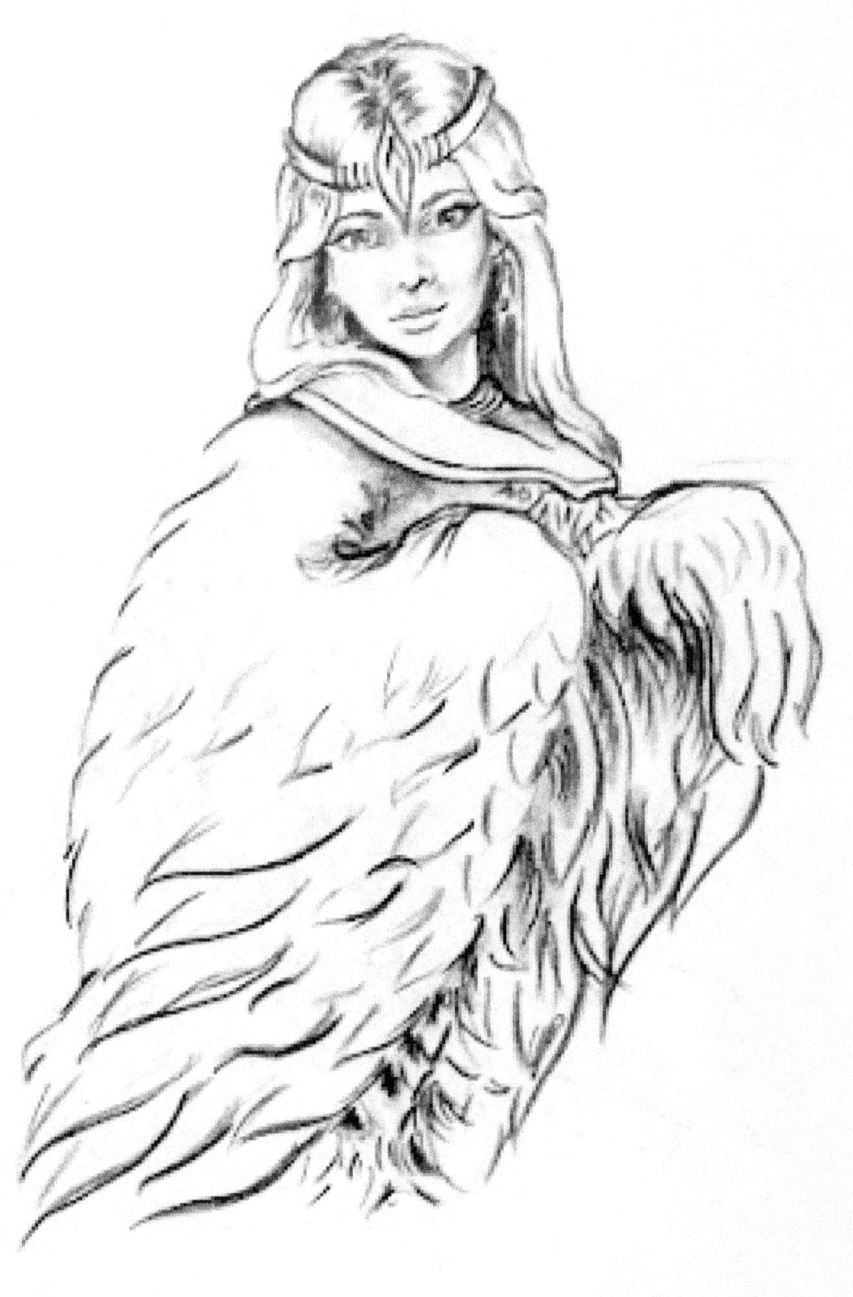

Here is the final drawing. Check and see if you need to draw in any final details you may have left out.

Chapter 3 – Beautiful young fairy

This young fairy is graceful and beautiful. She is clutching a blanket as if she has just awoken to behold a new day.

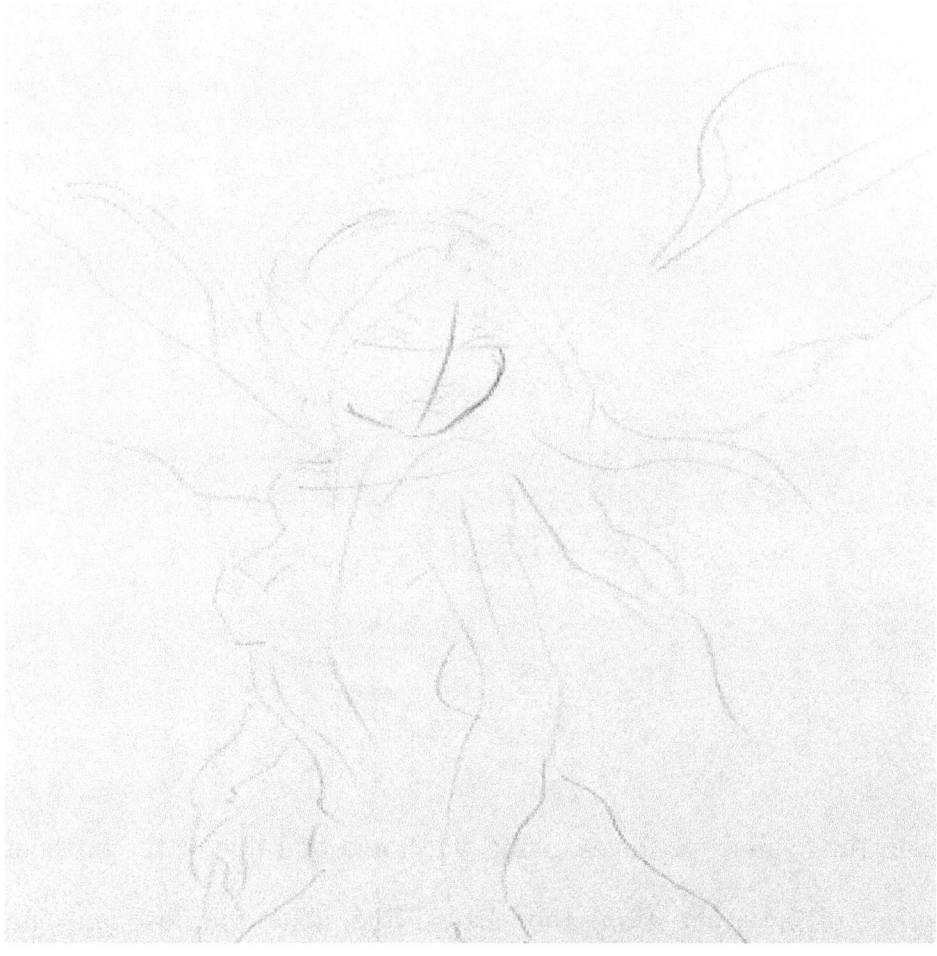

Draw the curved outline of the figure and the irregular markings that will become her wings. Make long, curved lines for her hair and long, tube-like arms and skinny torso. In the middle of the face, make a cross shape to help with the spacing of the facial features.

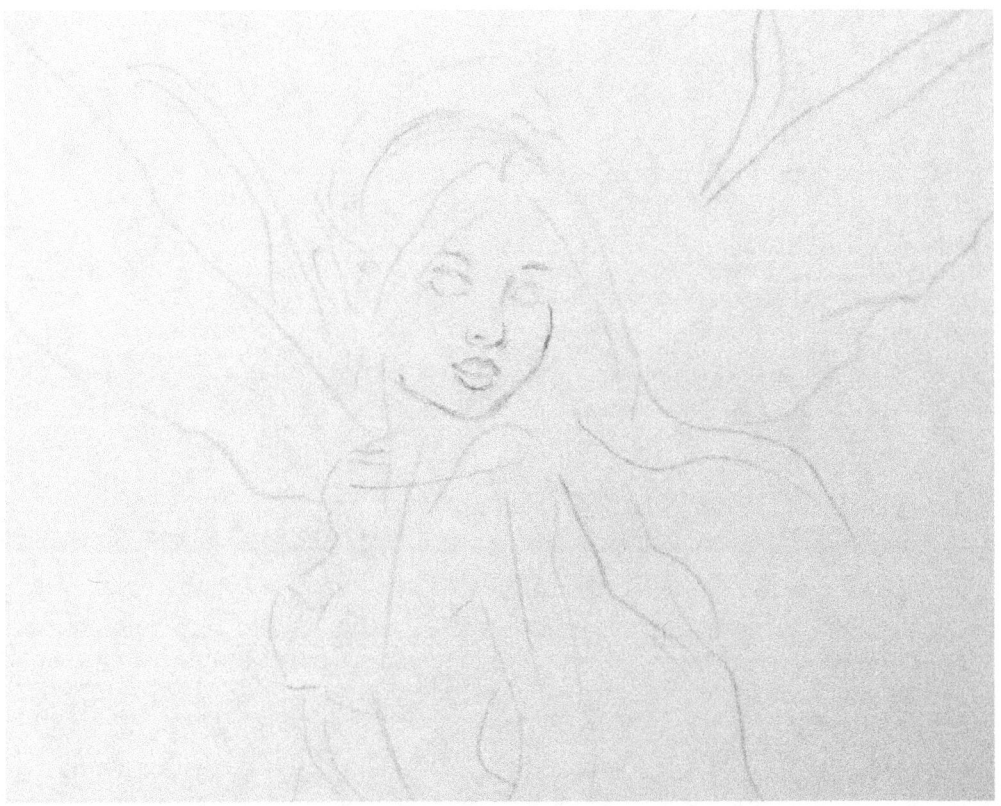

Draw in the oval-shaped eyes, using the horizontal line of the cross as the centerline of the ovals. Along the vertical line, make the nose and beneath this, the pointed, oval shape of the mouth and a curved line for the bottom lip. Erase the cross shape.

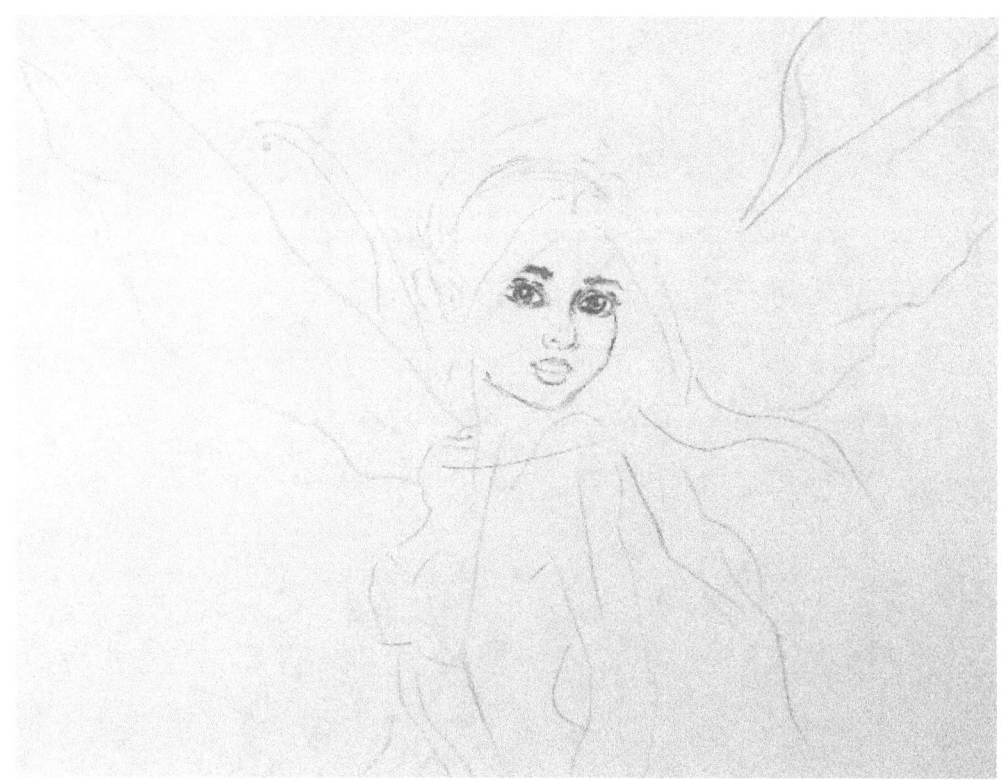

Go over the eyebrows with dark shading. Do the same around the outline of

the eyes. Shade in the iris of her eyes with dark markings and leave a small

circle unshaded inside the eyes.

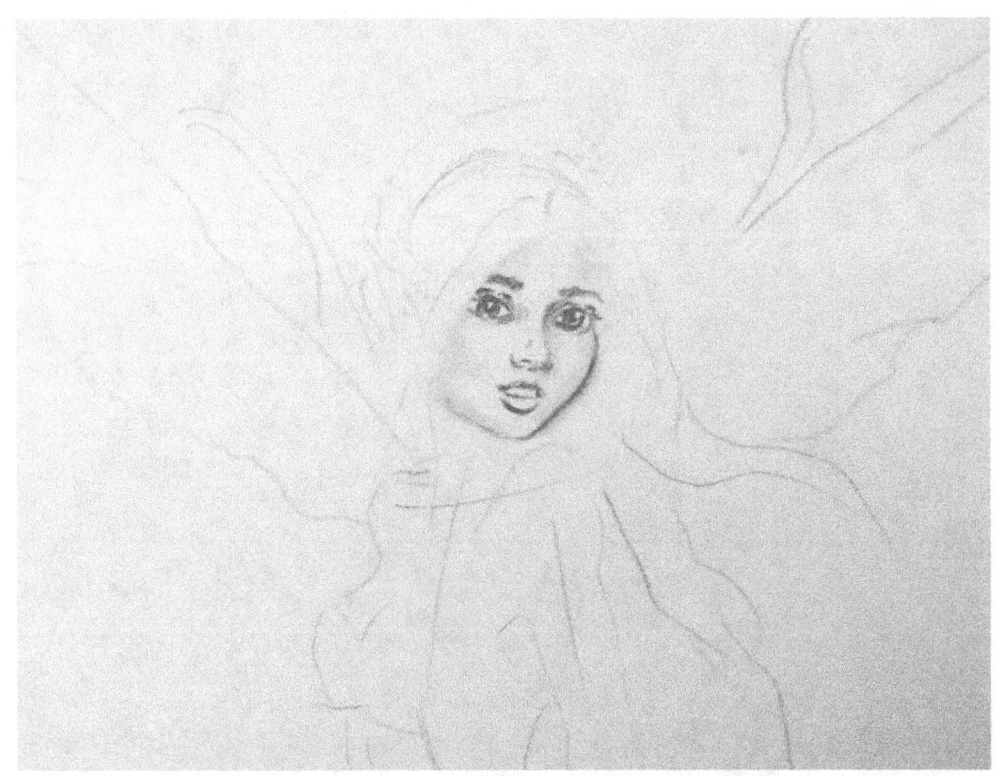

Make a dark line along the left edge of the face. Add some very subtle shading above the eyes and along both sides of the face.

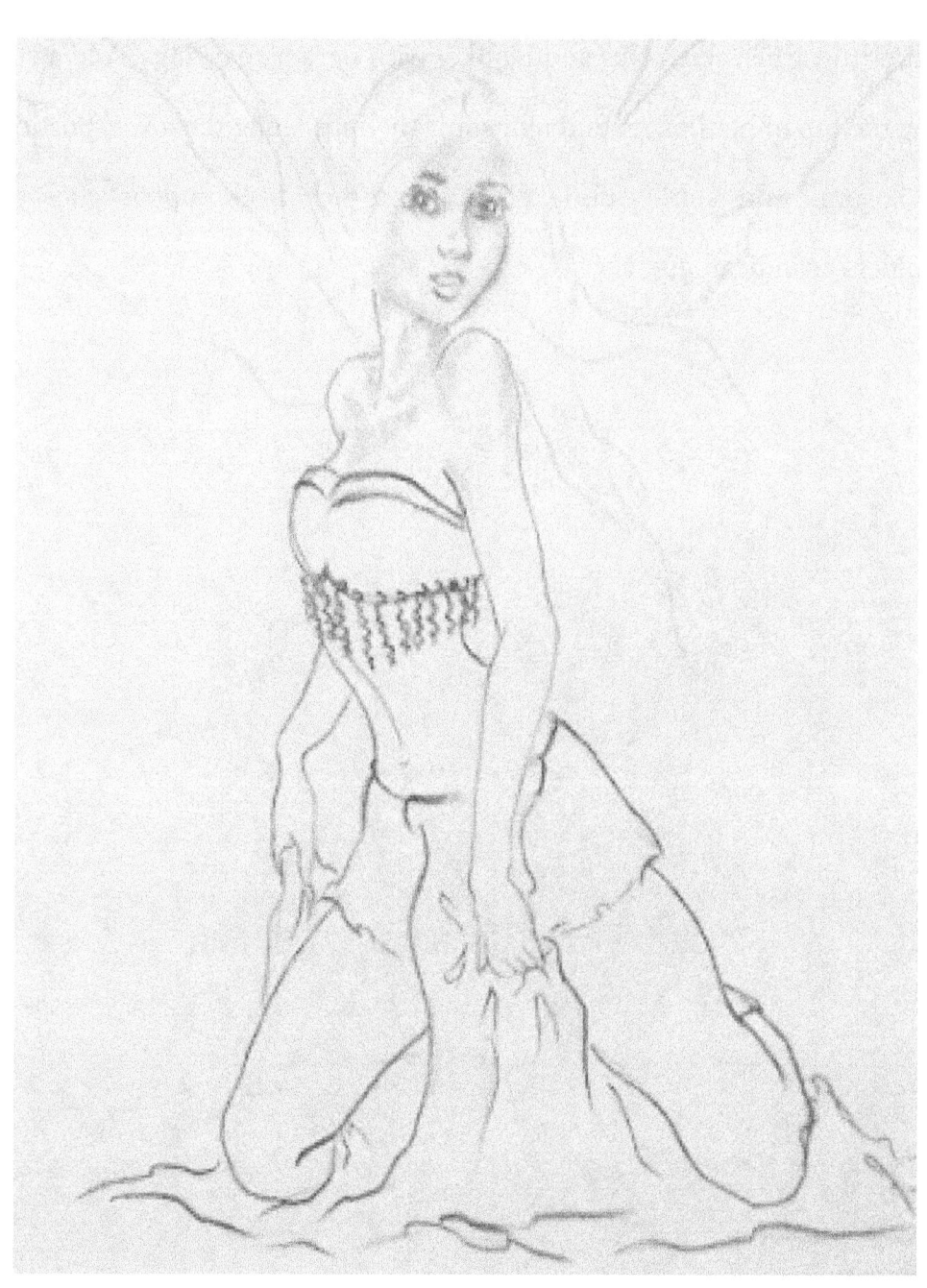

Go over the arms, skirt, legs and blanket with darker markings. Add a stripe along the top of her bosom and add squiggly lines along the lower portion of her bosom. Add some subtle shading on her neck, upper chest and shoulders as indicated.

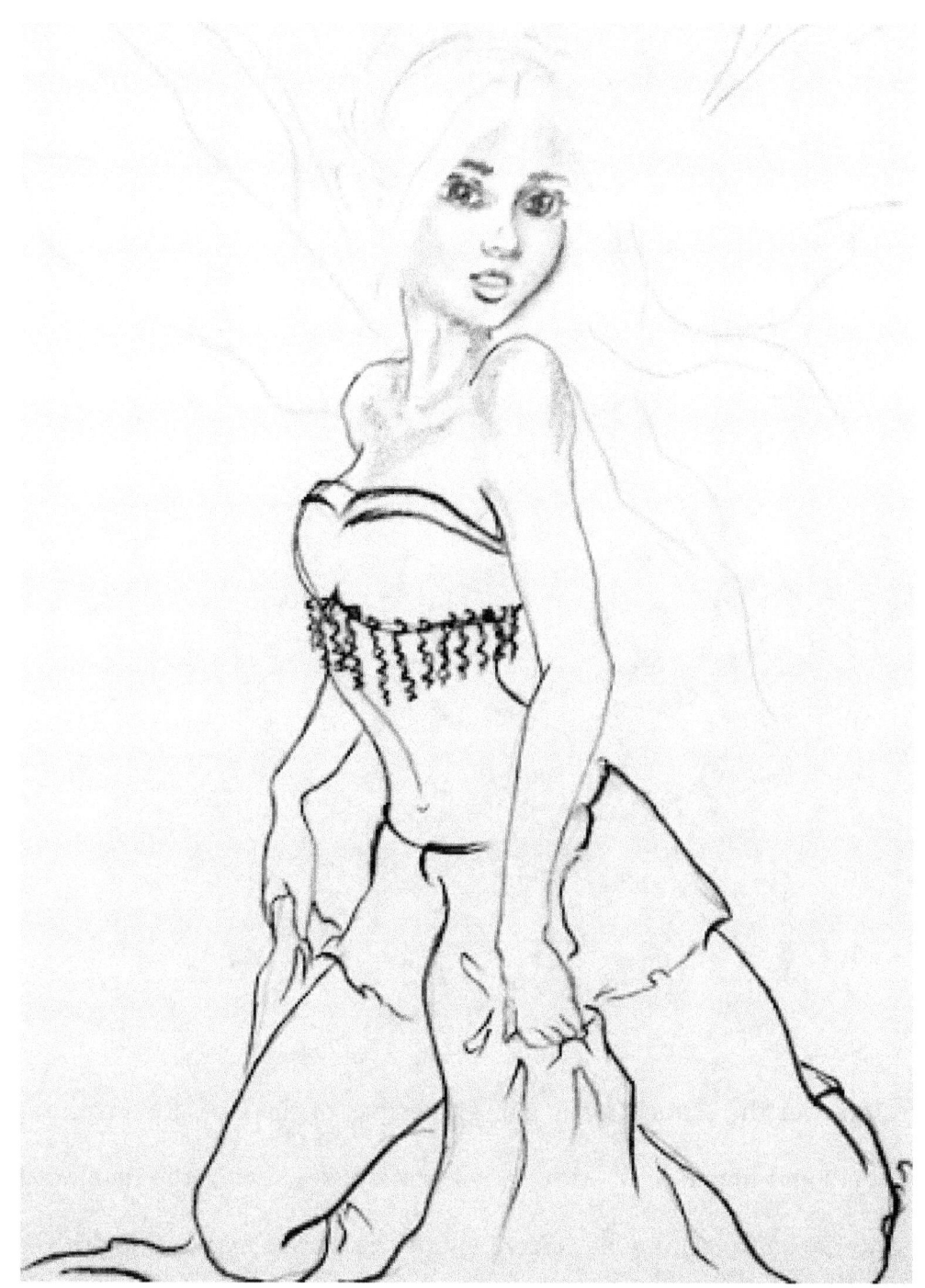

Here is a close up to help you add in the detailed shading along the neck, chest and shoulders.

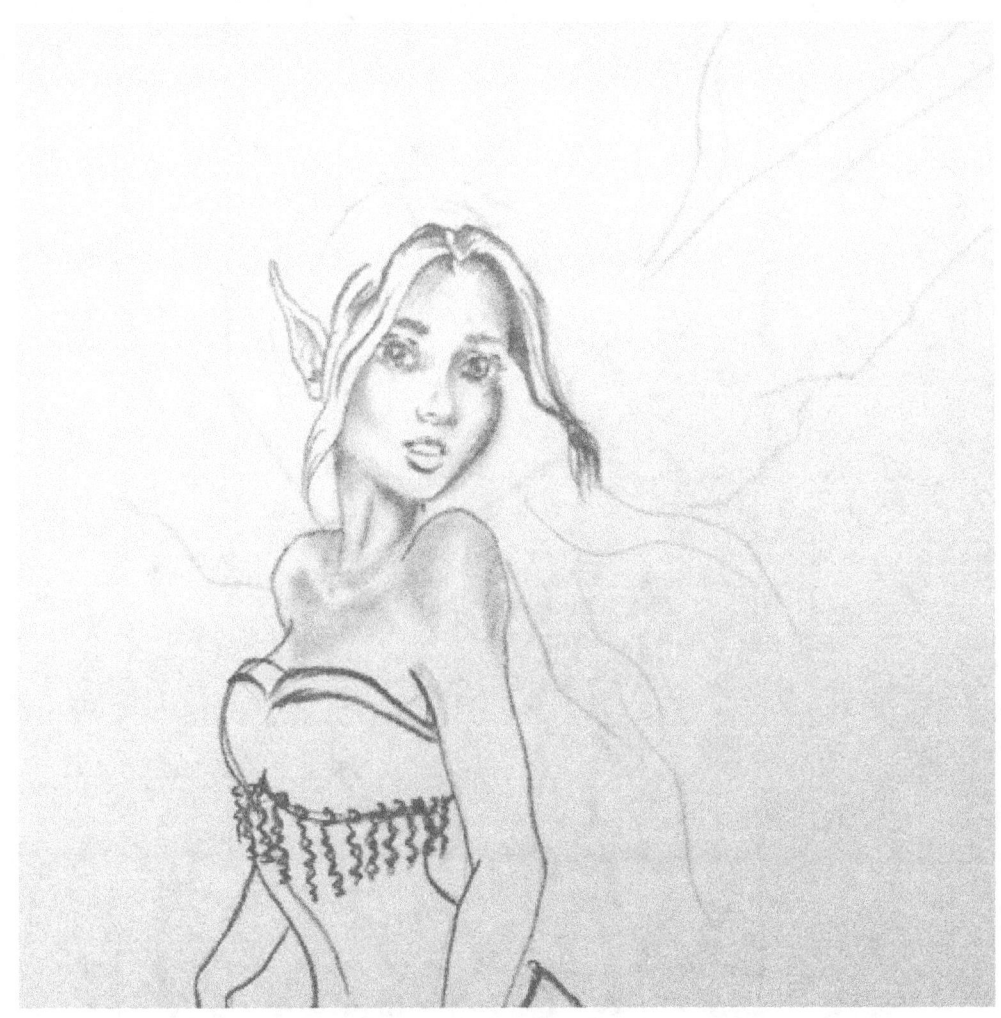

Now, go over the shaded areas along the sides of the face, forehead, neck, shoulders and upper chest with darker markings. Draw in the detail of her ear and the hair outlining her face. Include the darker marks along the edge of the left side of her hair.

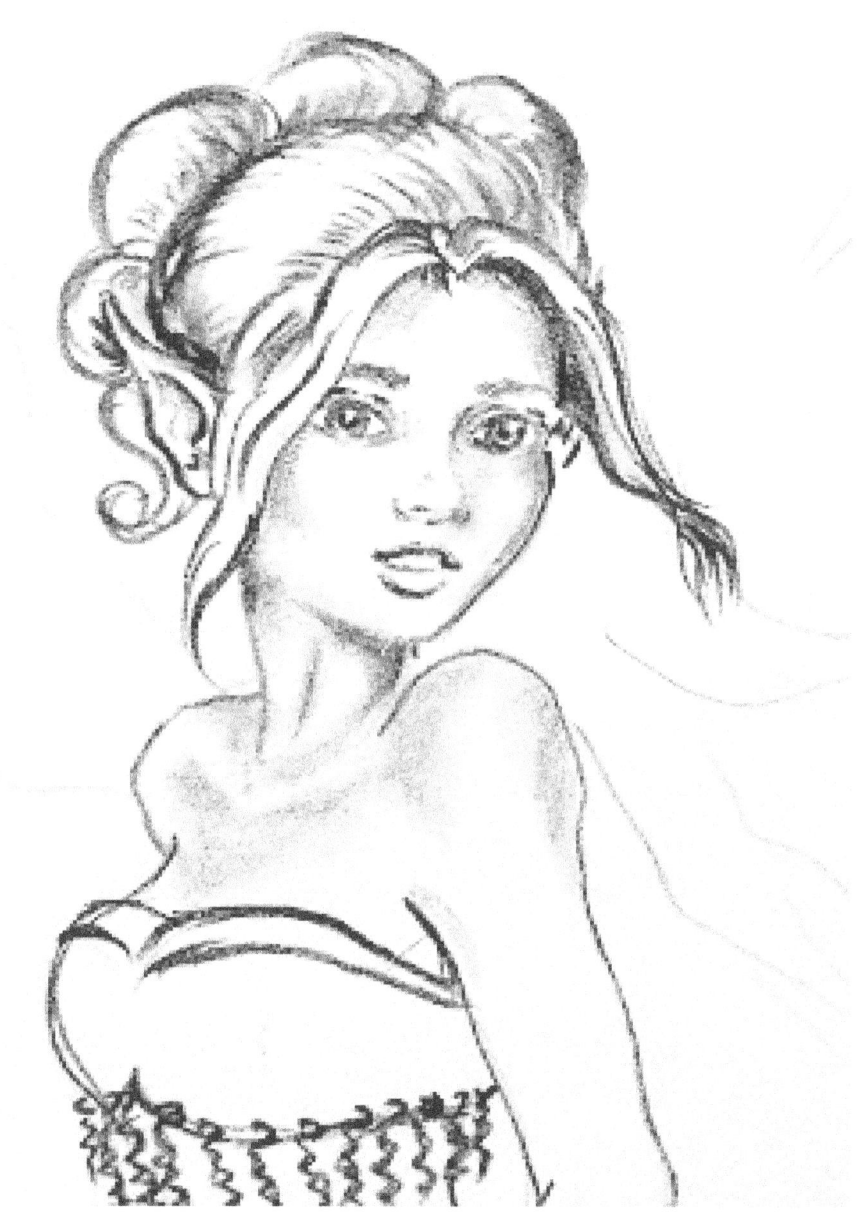

Draw in three, round shapes for the top of the hair and a large, round shape beneath this for the middle portion of the hair. Add in the curved marks within these shapes for hair and include some subtle shading as indicated in the drawing.

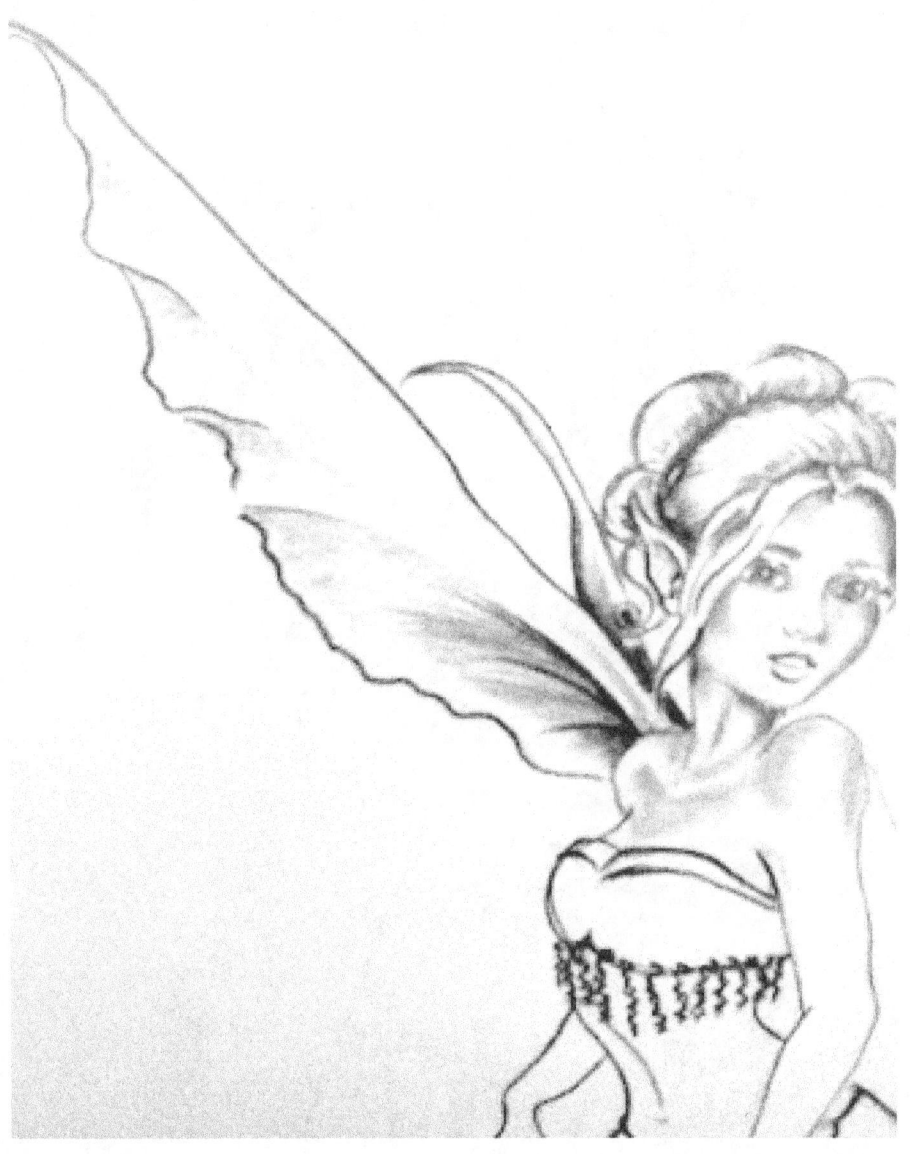

Go over the shape of the right wing with darker marks. Add the 'v' shaped regions of subtle shading on the lower portions of the wings, making sure that the curved lines and shading are darker where the wing meets the shoulder.

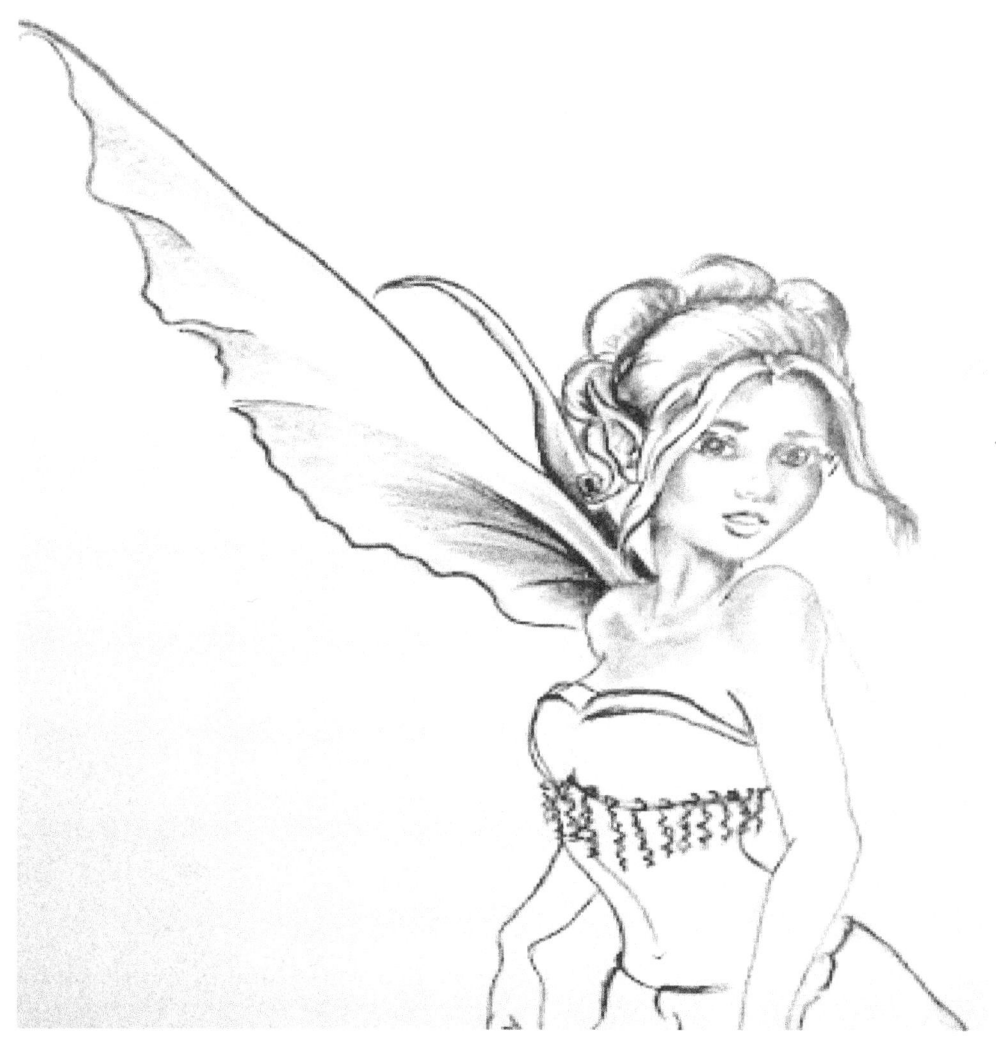

Add in the long, curved shape of her hair between her head and the right wing. Add darker shading along the bottom of this and a small, round region beneath the ear.

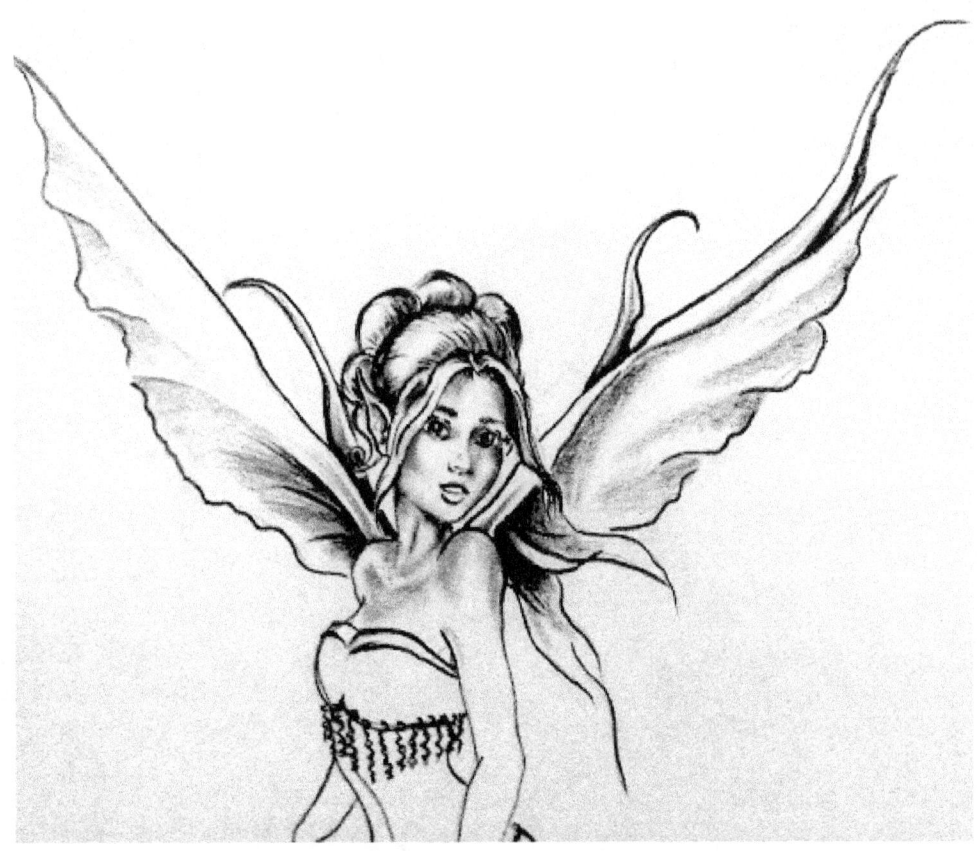

Go over the edge of the left wing and add in the regions of subtle shading along the edges. Make sure to make the shading very dark near the left shoulder for contrast. Add in the other curved shapes above and below the left wings as well.

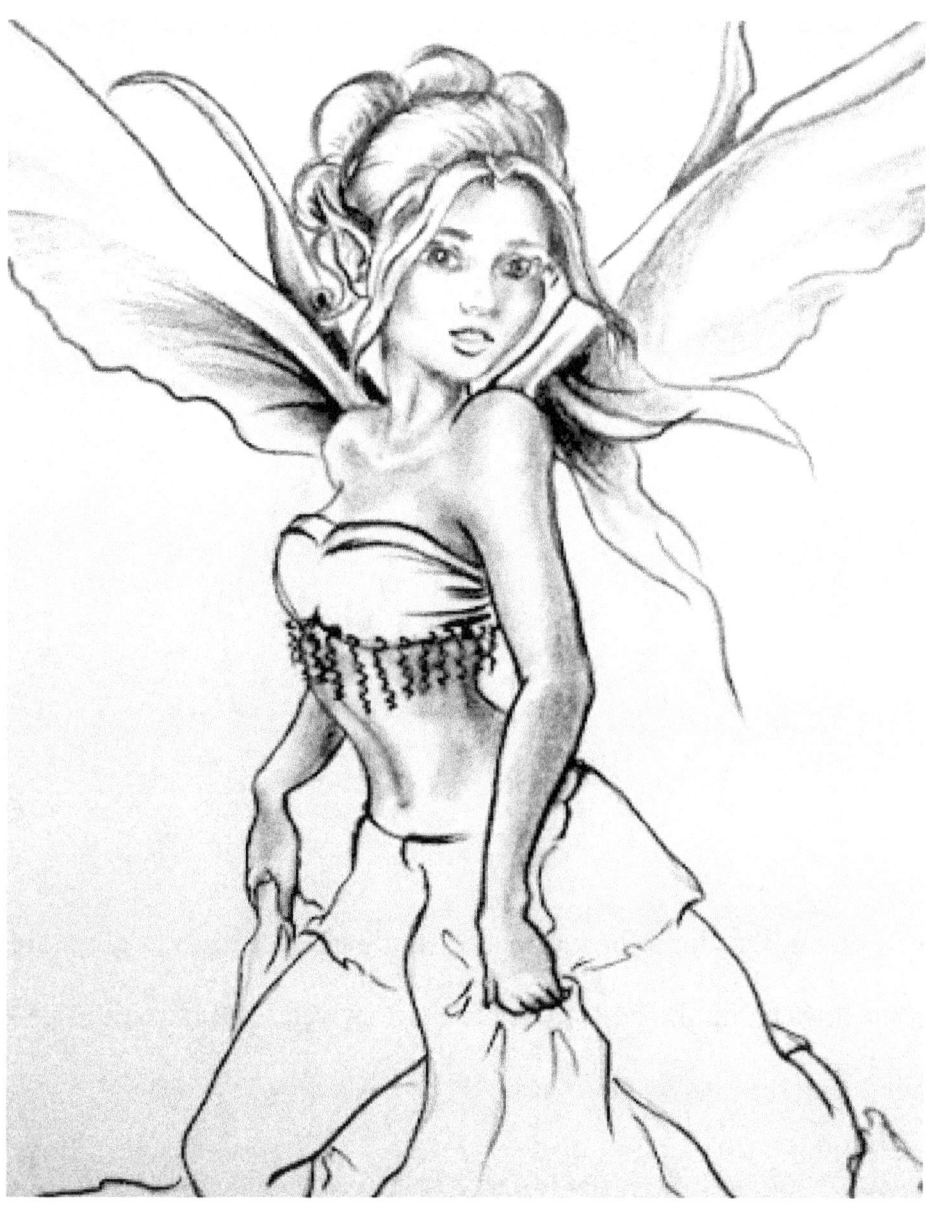

Add in subtle shading along the arms and belly of the figure.

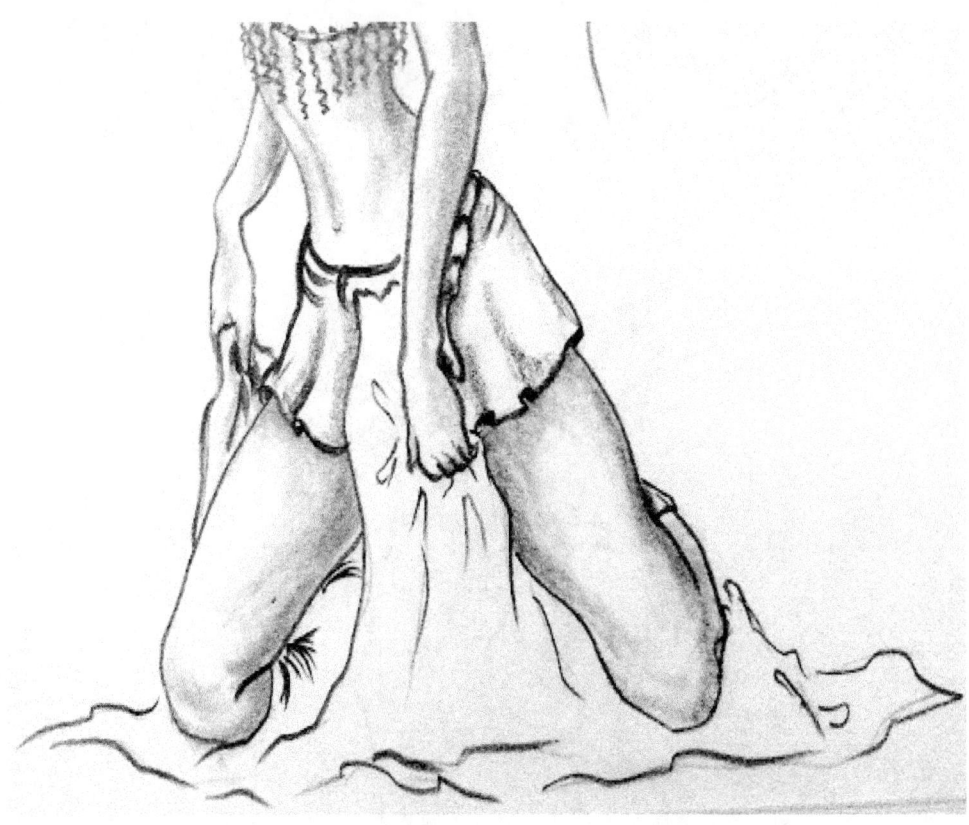

Draw in the marks along the waste and shade in the ruffles in her skirt. Add in darker lines along the bottom of her skirt as well. Add in regions of subtle shading along the edges of her legs.

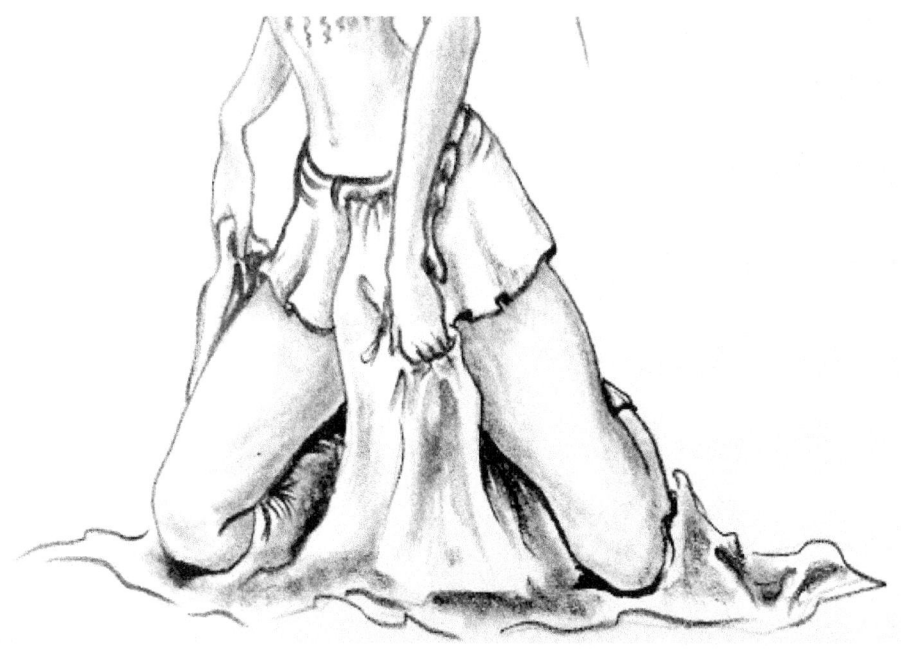

Add in the curved lines and shaded regions of the blanket. Make sure to use very dark shading along the region where her legs touches the blanket.

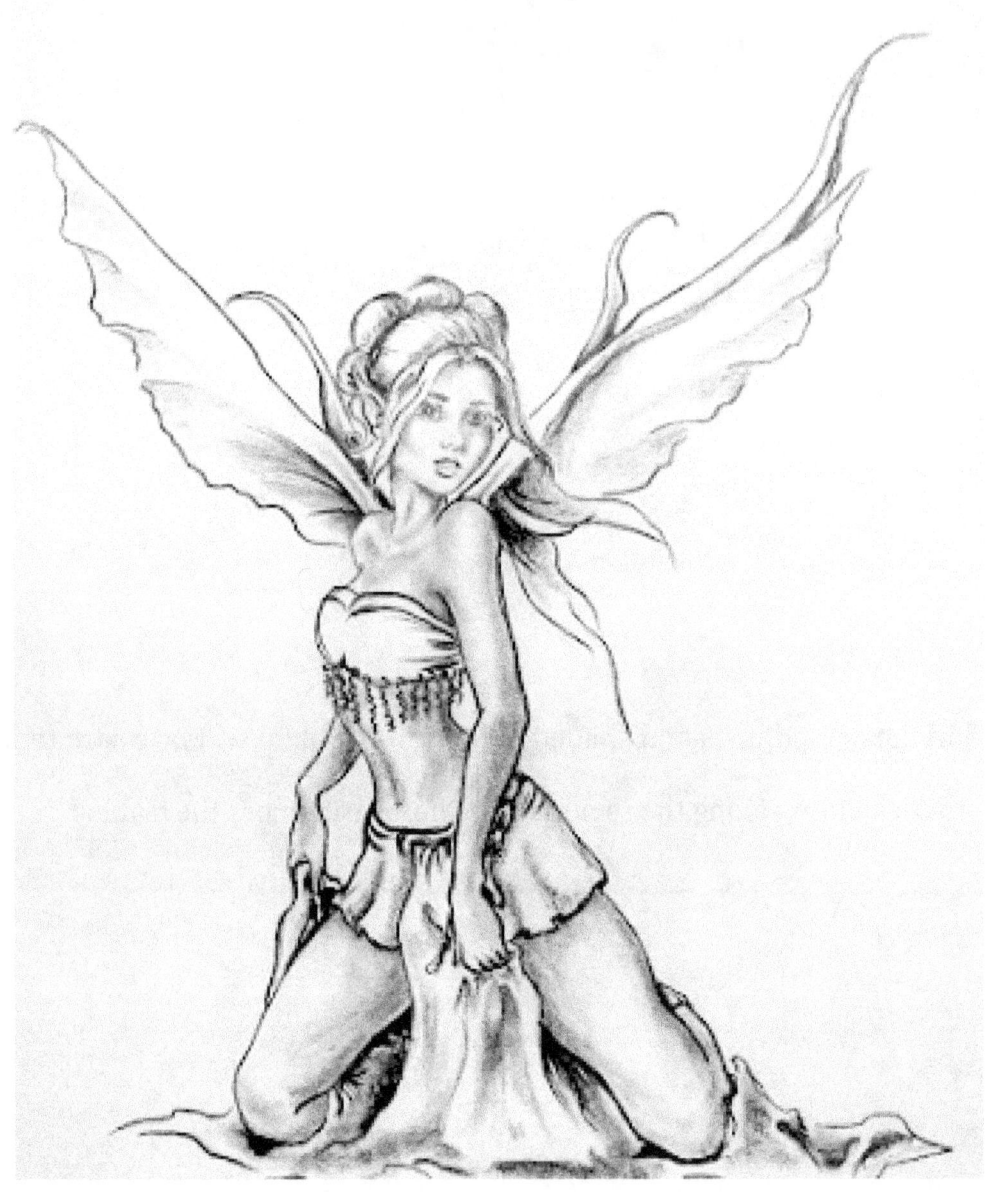

Here is a full view of the figure. Now check the details to see if there's anything that you may have left out.

Chapter 4 – Fairy Enchantress

This fairy has her arm extended as if she is casting a spell or working her magic. Her stature and posture show that she has great powers that she will use towards good ends.

Draw an hourglass shape that will become the body; and the head, looking towards the right. Draw the right arms extended outwards. Add in the wings with smooth, curved wings on the top and pointed edges on the inside.

Add in the curved lines on the wings. Lightly, sketch the eyes, nose and mouth and the curved lines on the neck and top of her gown.

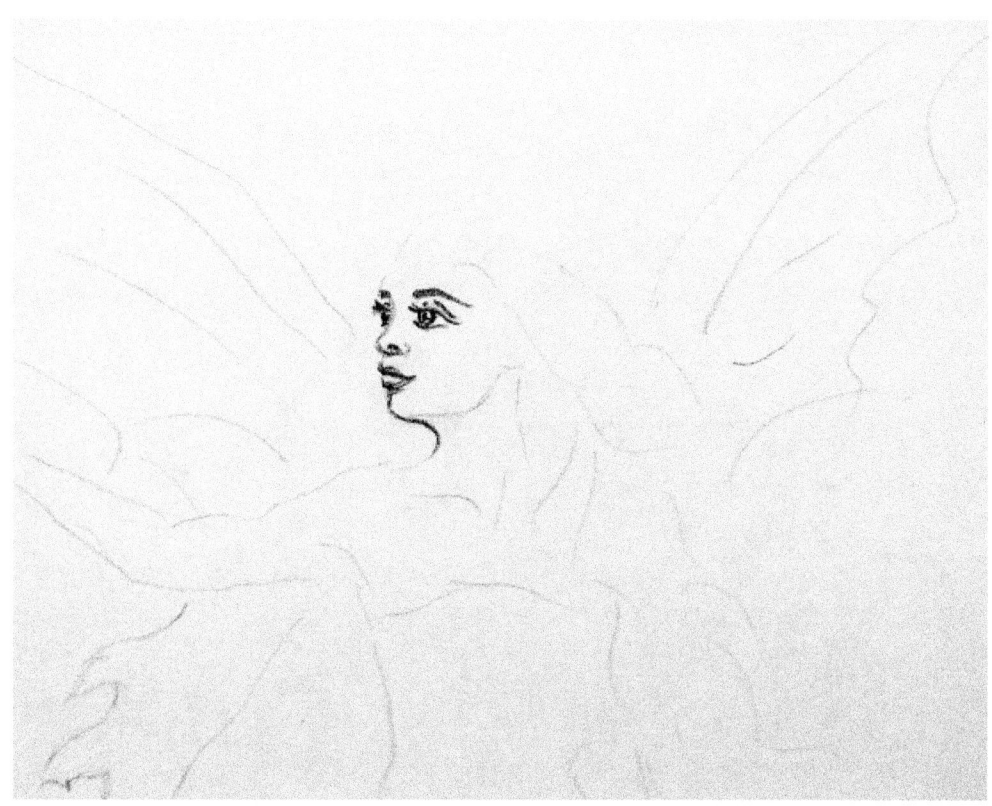

Draw the eyebrows in with very dark shading. Make a small curved line on the top and bottom of the left eye and a small circle for her pupil. With darker marks, draw in her nostril and lips, making a dark line for her mouth opening.

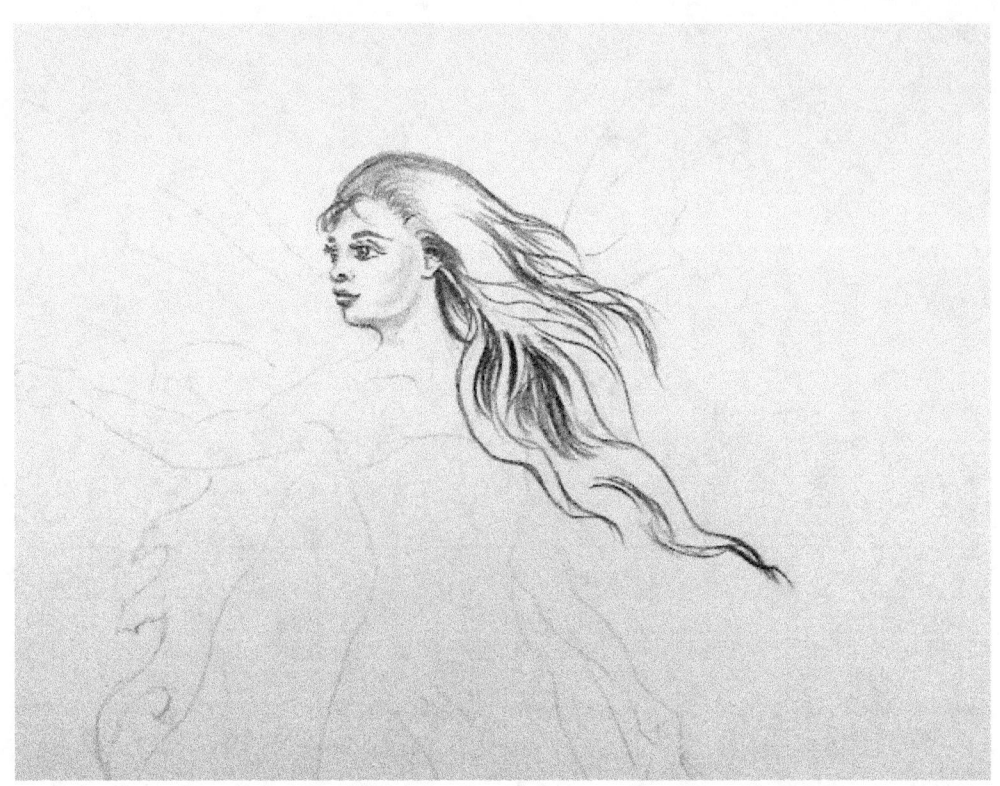

Sketch long, curved lines to make up the hair. Make sure some regions of her hair are darker as indicated in the drawing. Leave an area in the center without curved lines as indicated.

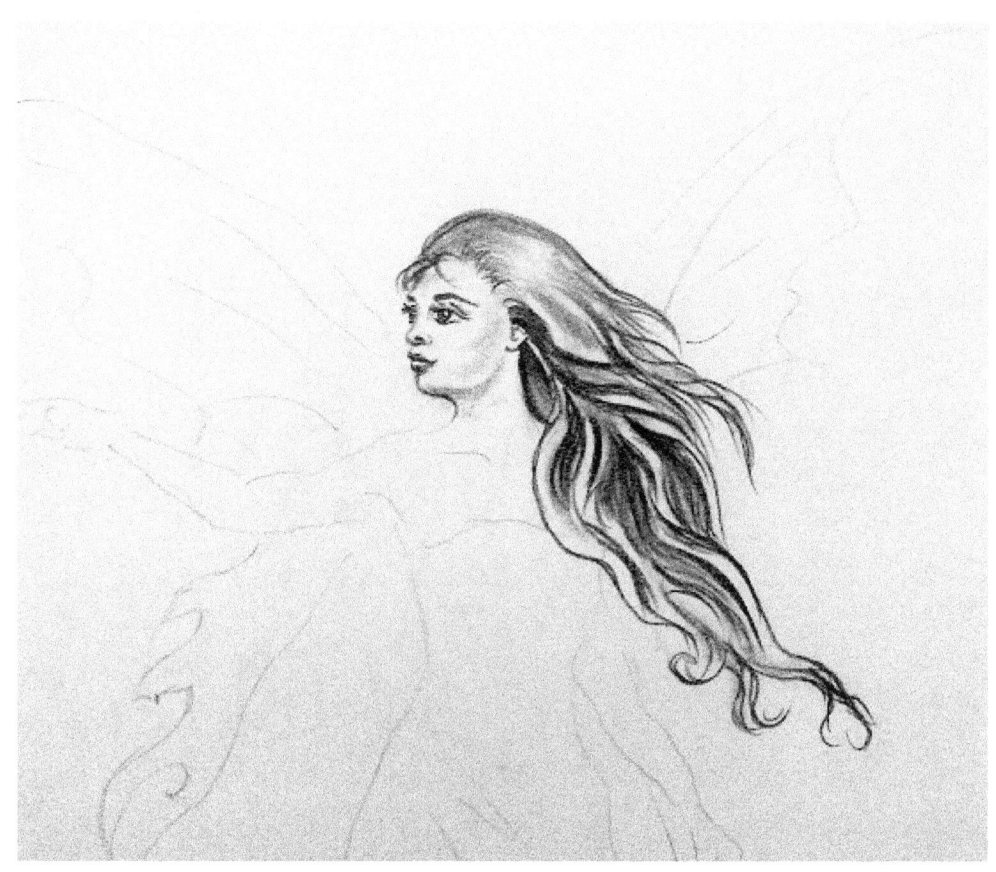

Add in more regions of shading with darker, curved lines, leaving some areas of her hair unshaded.

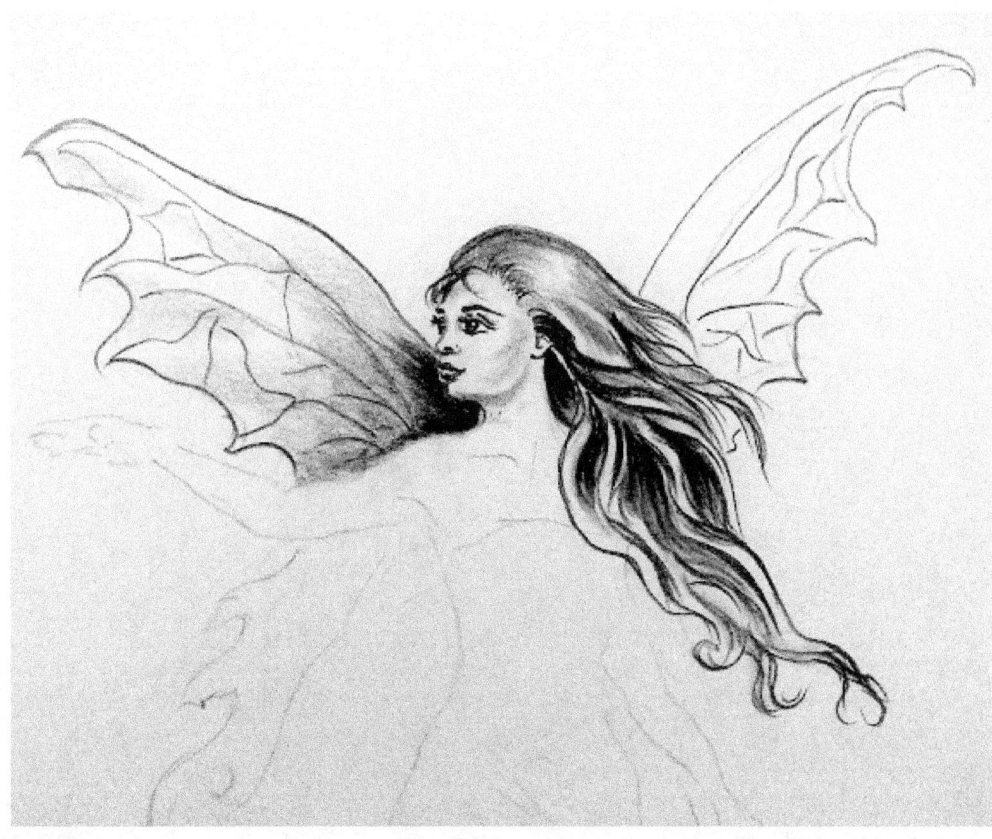

Put the curved, irregular lines inside of the left and right wings. Do some really dark shading on the left edge of the right wing. Add lighter shading extending form the darker region.

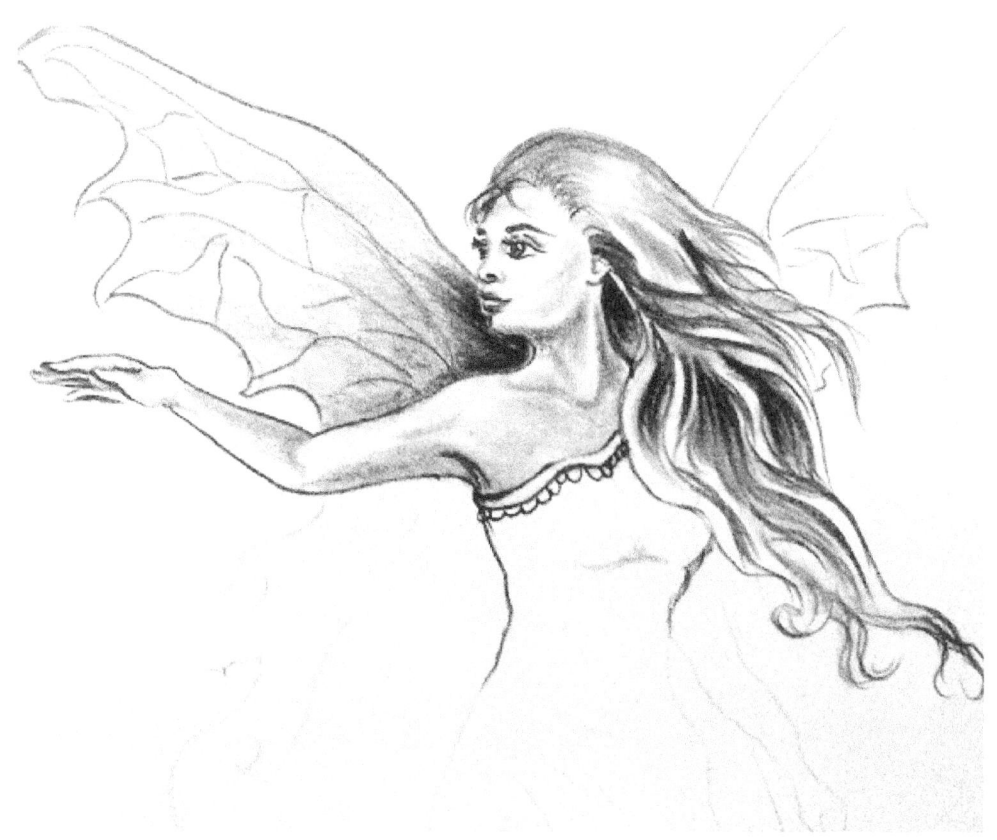

Add some subtle shading on the cheeks. Draw in some shading below the jaw line, making it darker just below the jawline and lighter as you extend downwards. Draw a curved line of shading along the bottom of the neck. Add some shading along the edges of the right arm. Draw in the line of trim outlining the top of her gown and line the top with semi-circular shapes.

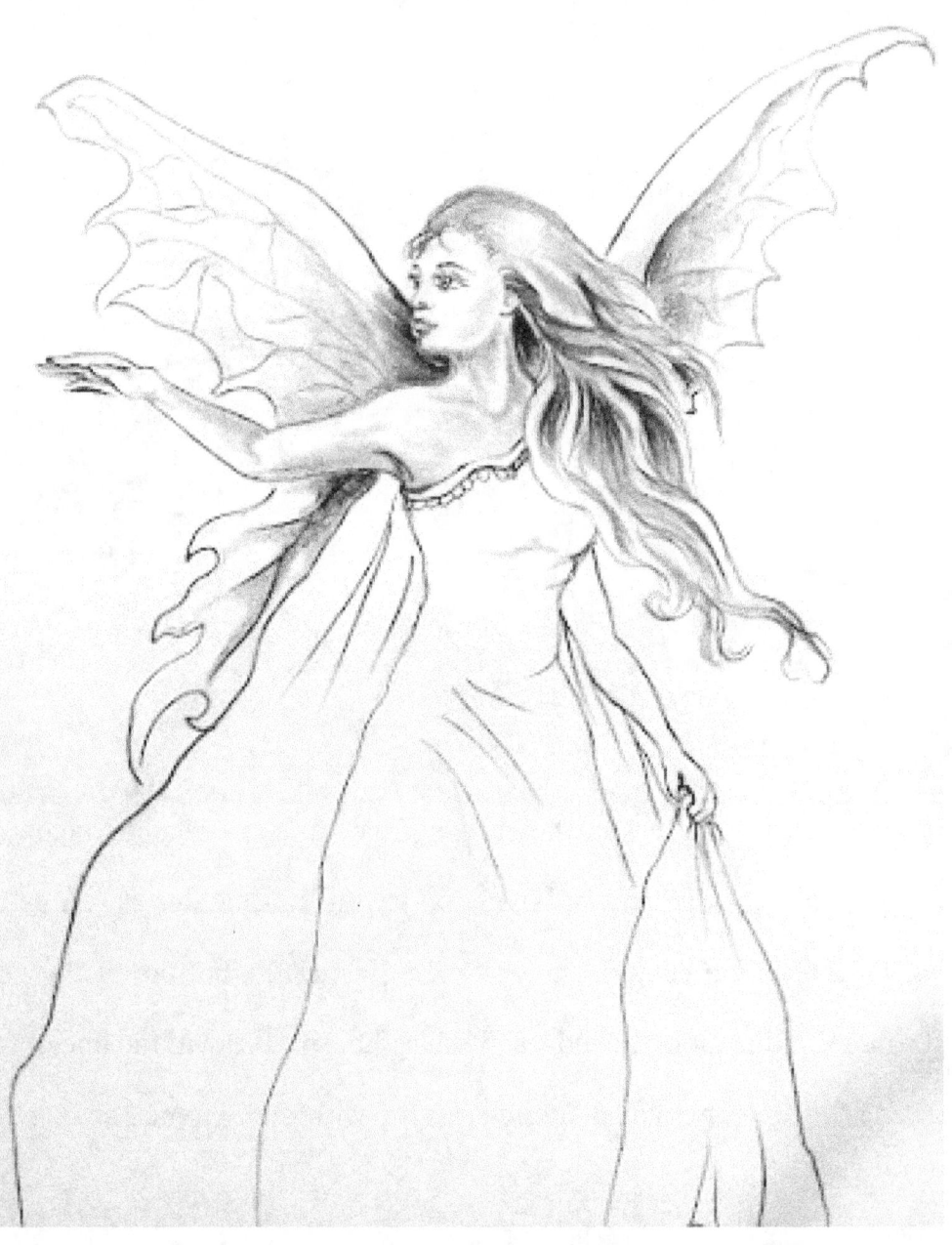

Draw the long, curved lines that make up the gown and include the curved lines that make up the ruffles. Draw in the lines in the bottom portion of the right wings and shade this portion of the wing in along the line in the center, making it darker at the top.

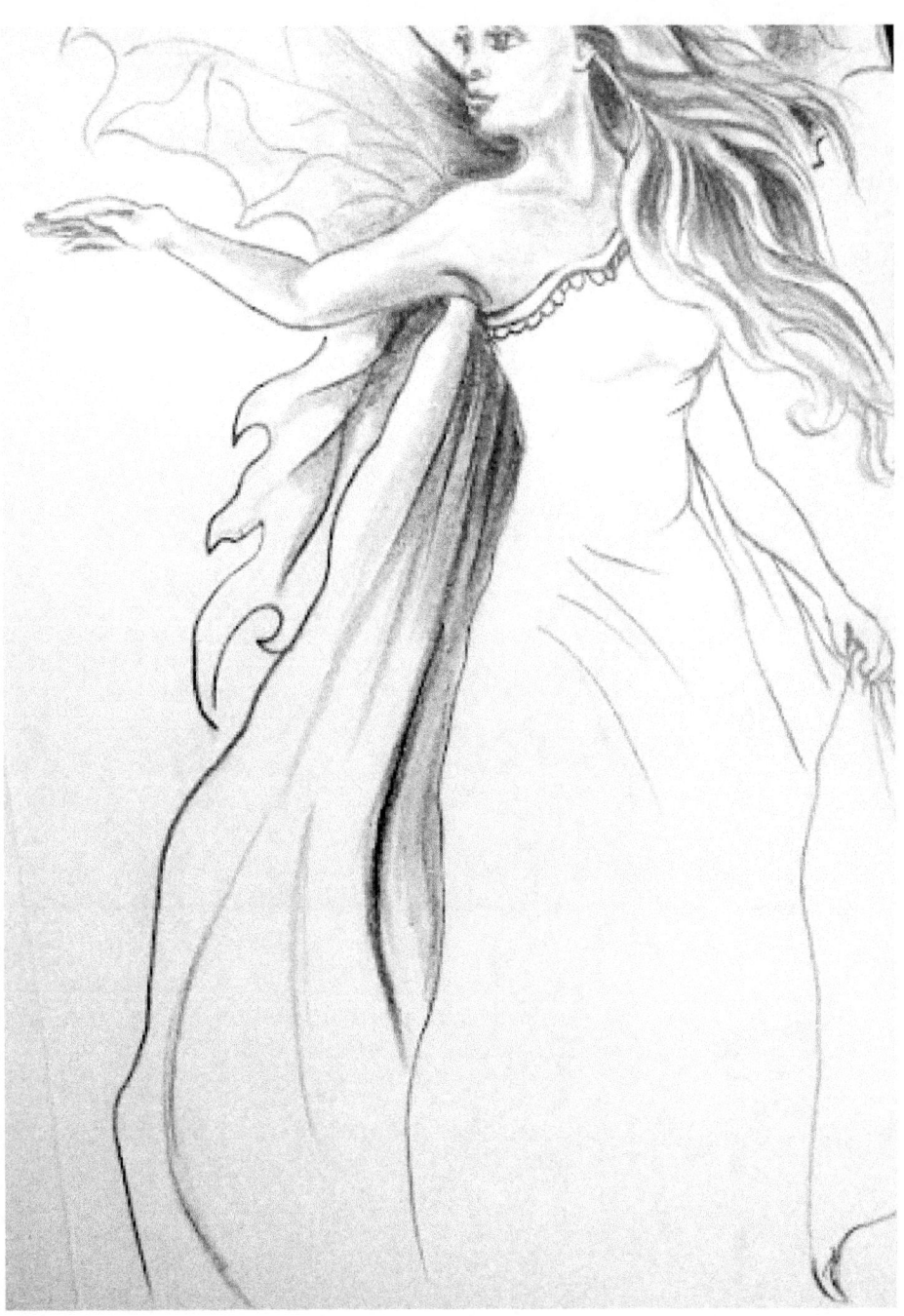

Add some dark lines on the right side of the gown, extending downwards.

Do some shading in this region that is darker towards the top and becomes

lighter as it extends downward.

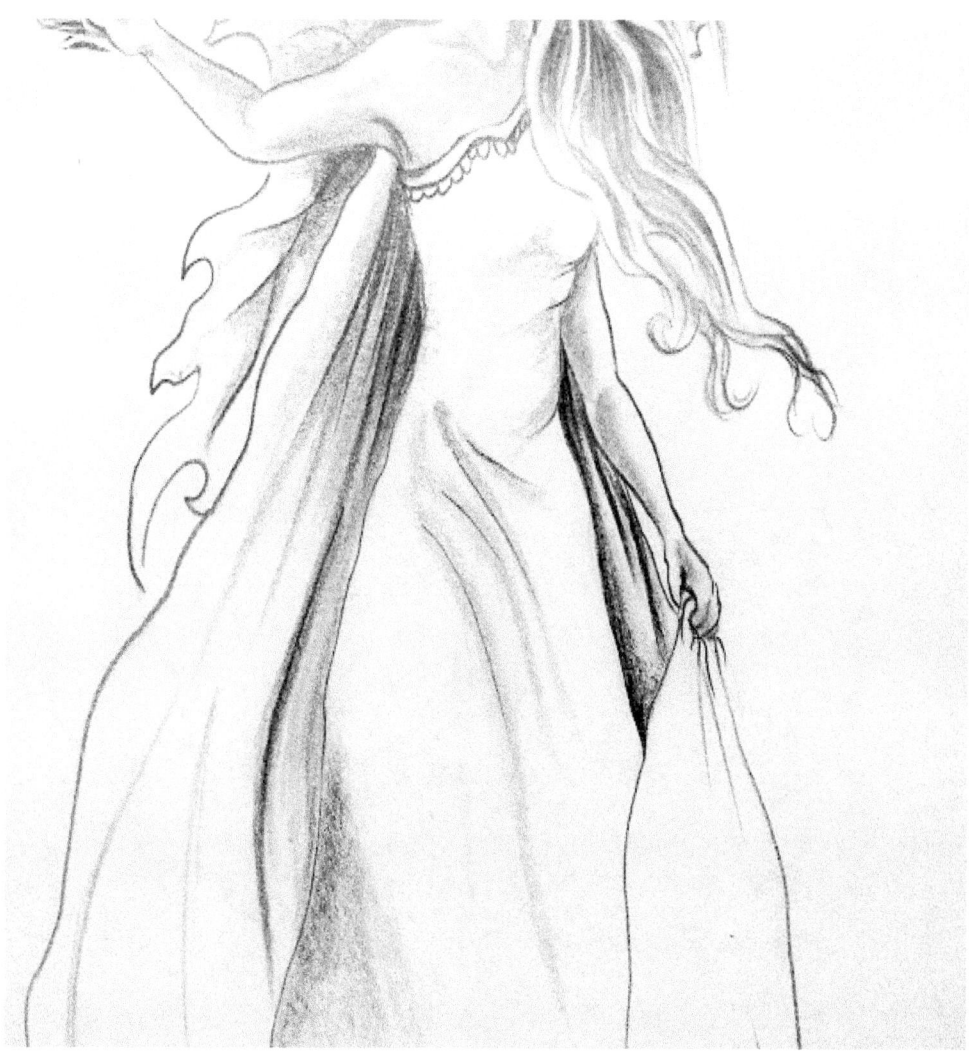

Add some subtle shading along the crease lines in the middle portion of the gown and along the bottom, center region of the gown. Add some shading along the creases in the torso region of the gown and along the left arm. Now, add some darker shading in the area to the right of the left arm.

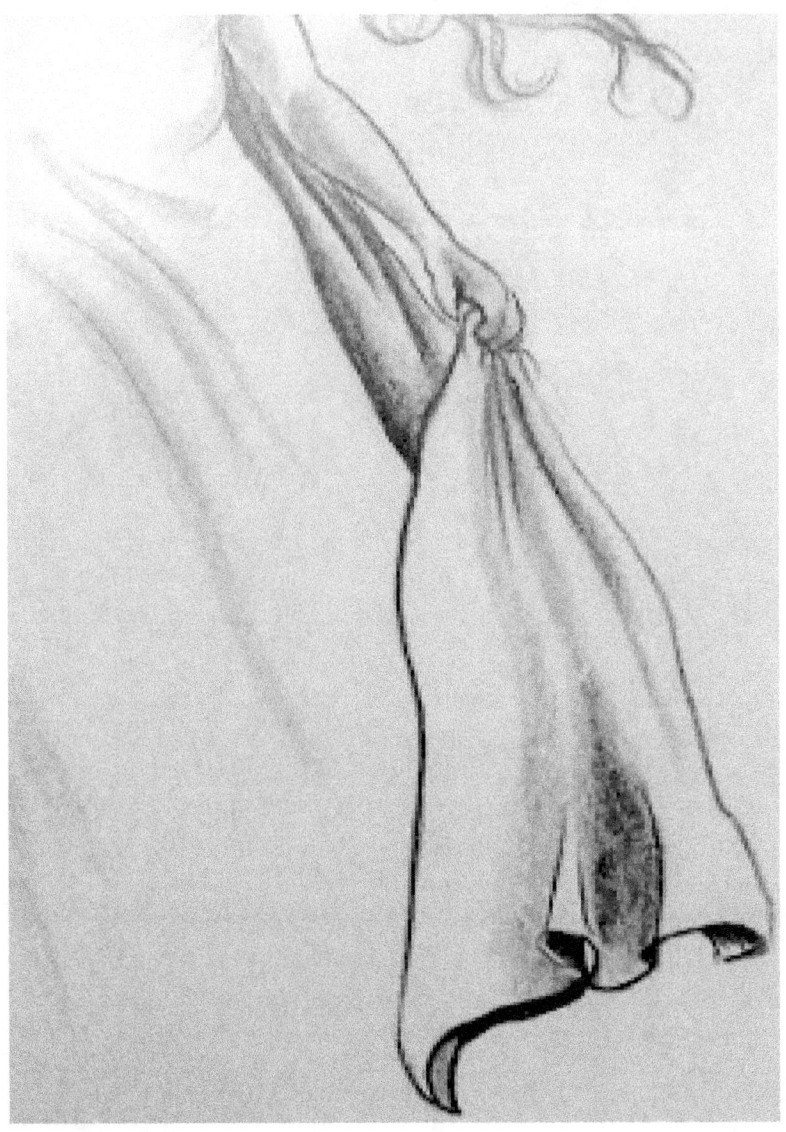

Along the bottom of the left side of the gown, make a curved line with a narrow loop and wider loop. Do some shading along the bottom that is darker in the center portion and inside the first loop. Add a triangular shape extending up from the first loop. Add some subtle shading in the region of the triangular lines you made and darker shading beneath the second loop.

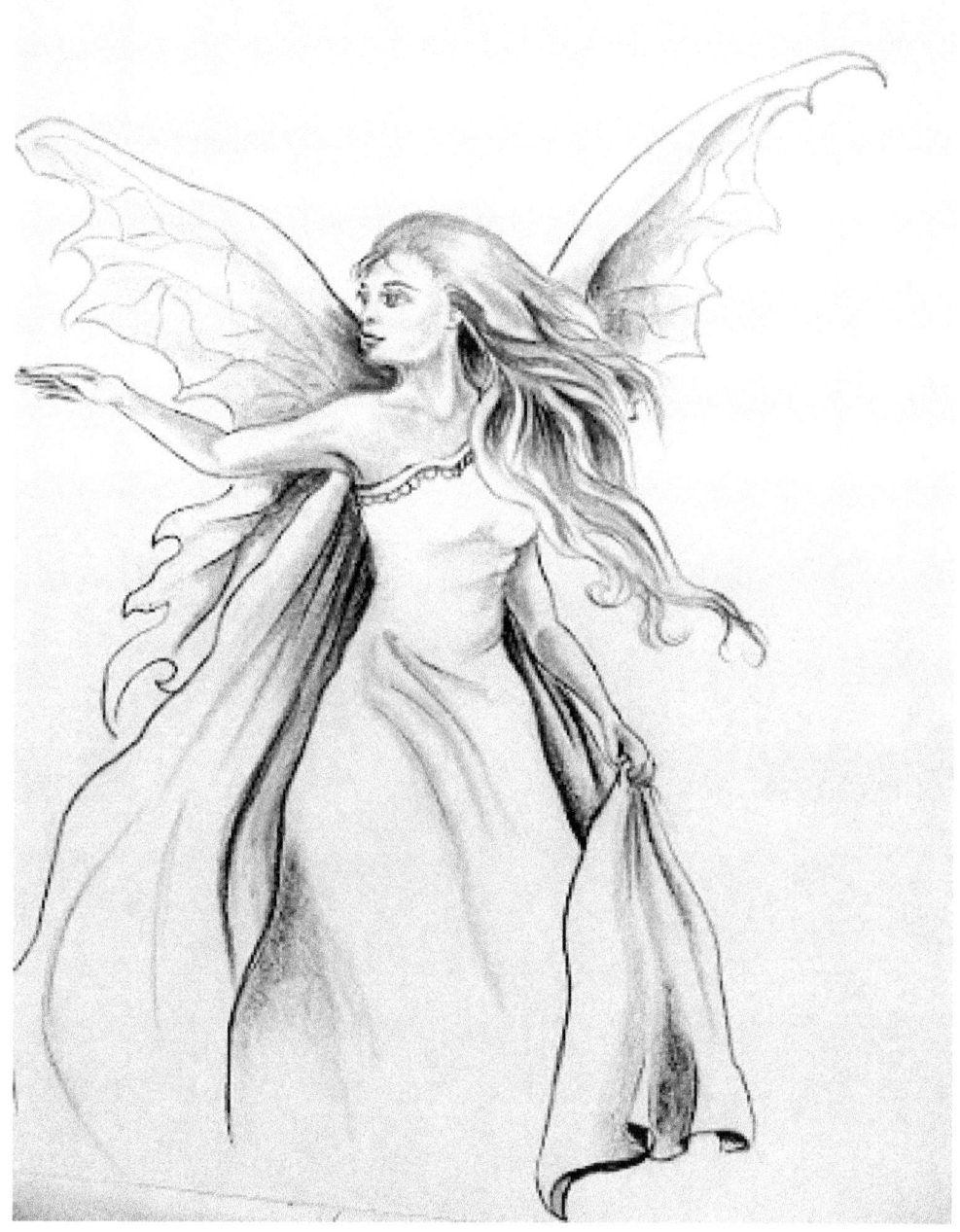

Here is the final drawing! If necessary, go back and add in any details you have missed. Pay particular attention to the creases in the gown and the regions of shading.

Chapter 5 – Young Angel

This young angel has a casual beauty. She is holding a magic elixir that she will use to heal someone who is in need. Her slight smile shows that she is friendly and anxious to help those who are less fortunate.

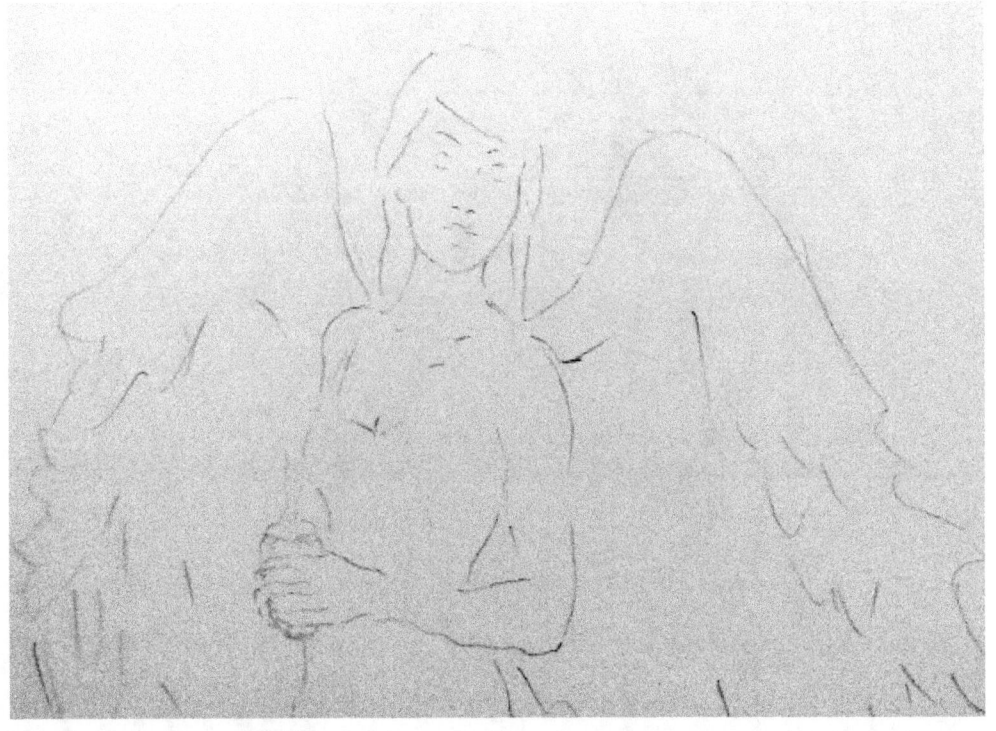

Draw the outline of the figure including the two wings and the figure in the center. Add the small marks on the wings. Now, make the outline of the angel's hair and the eyebrows, bridge of the nose, nostrils and curve of her lips. Below this, draw the left arm and the torso. In the hand, include a small can.

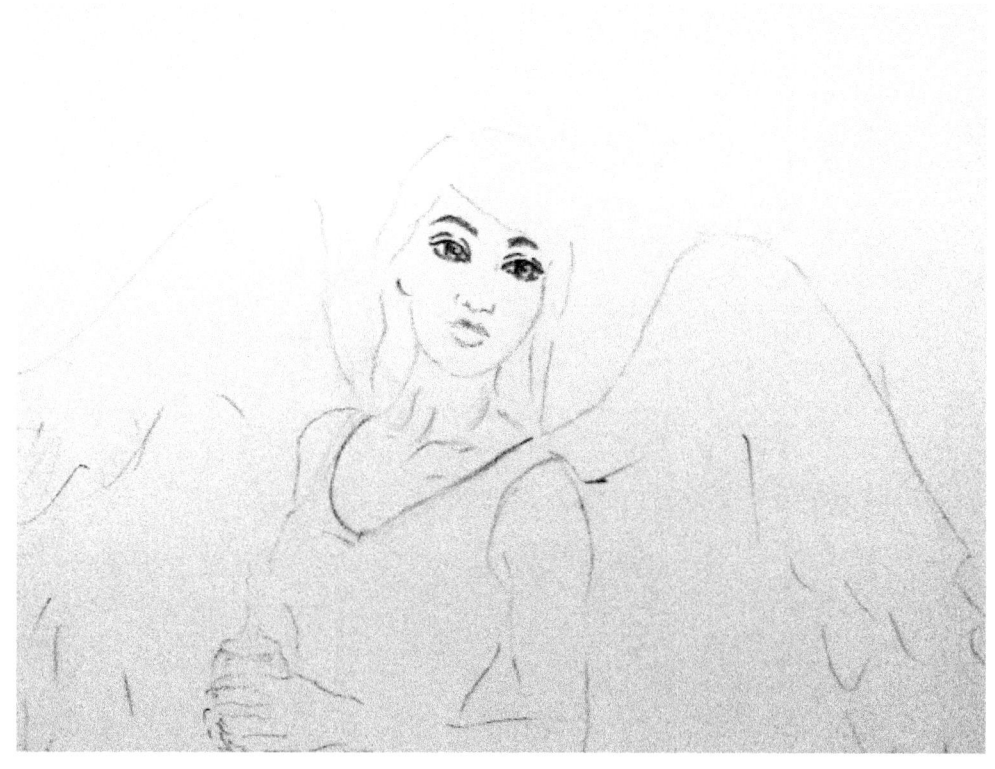

Use dark shading to draw in the eyebrows. Below this, make two point ovals that have a small circle inside of them. Add the small marks above the eye. Now draw the nose makes a flattened 'm' shape. Draw in full lips and lightly shade the top one. Add a few curved lines to form the neck and below this, add the low cut neck line of her shirt.

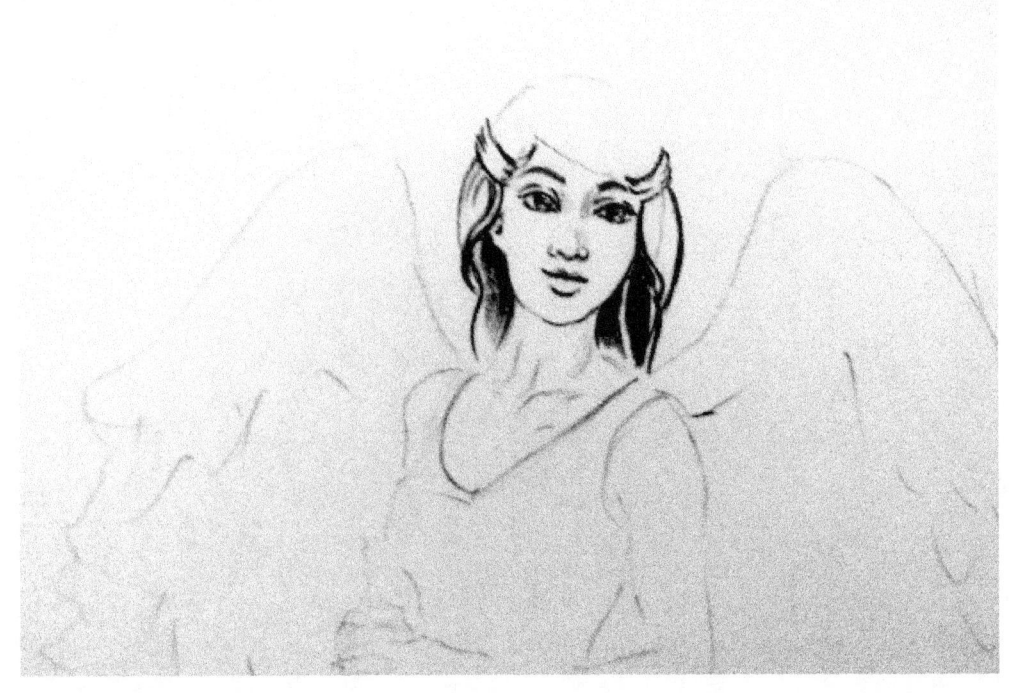

On either side of the figure's head, make two bands. Below this, draw the curved lines that make up her hair. Add some darker shading on the lower edges of her hair on both sides of her head. Go over her mouth with darker marks, adding a line in the center that curves upwards to suggest a slight smile.

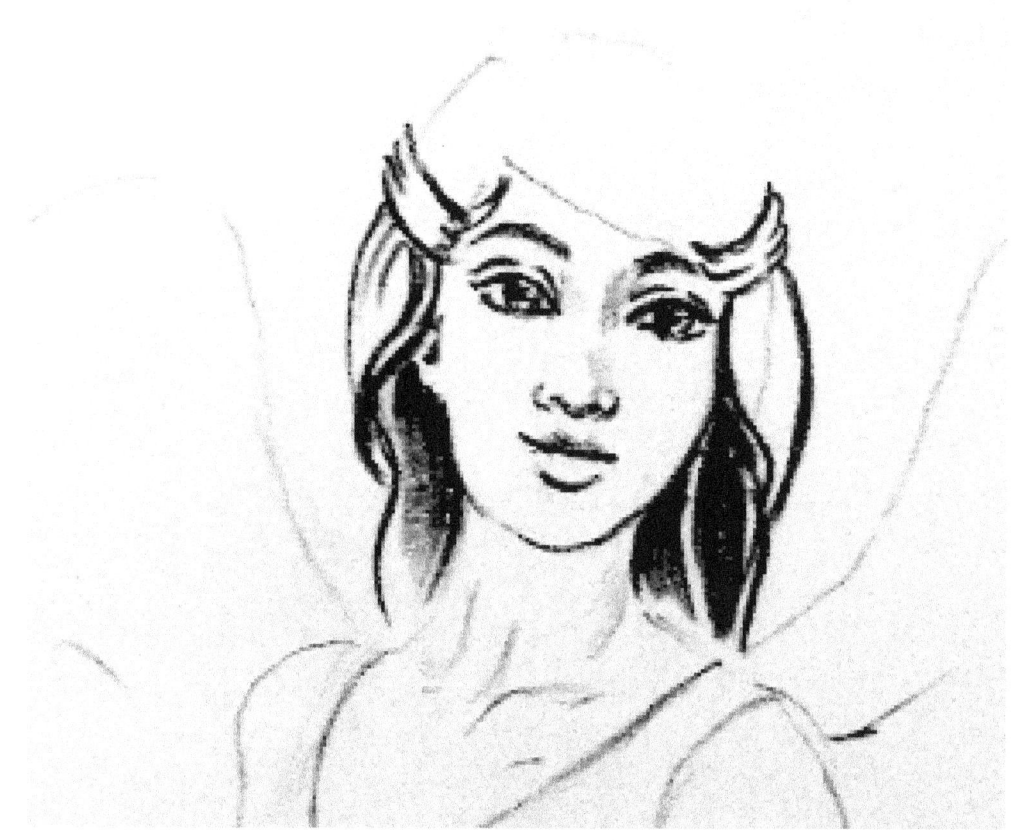

Add a little bit of light shading to the bridge of her nose.

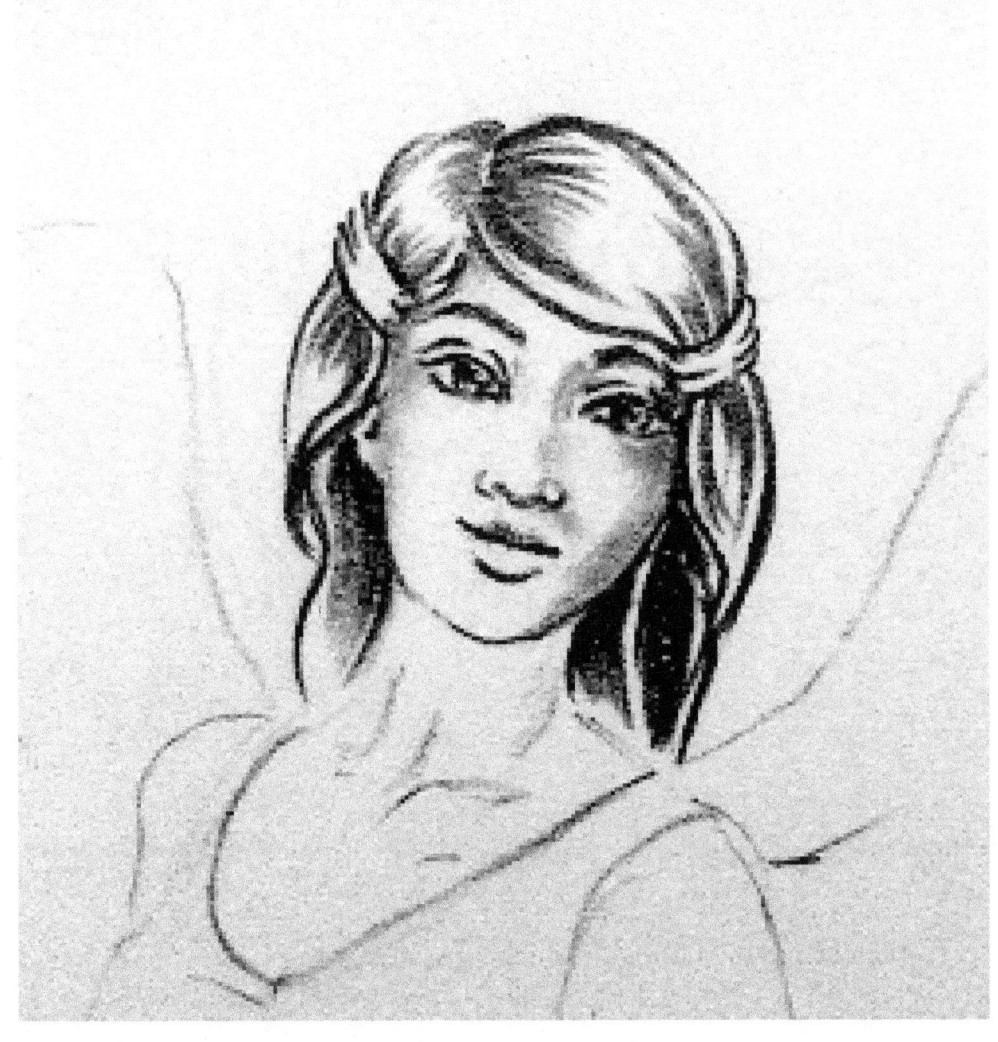

On the top of her head do some light shading that extends from her hairline as indicated in the picture. Add some light shading on both sides of the face.

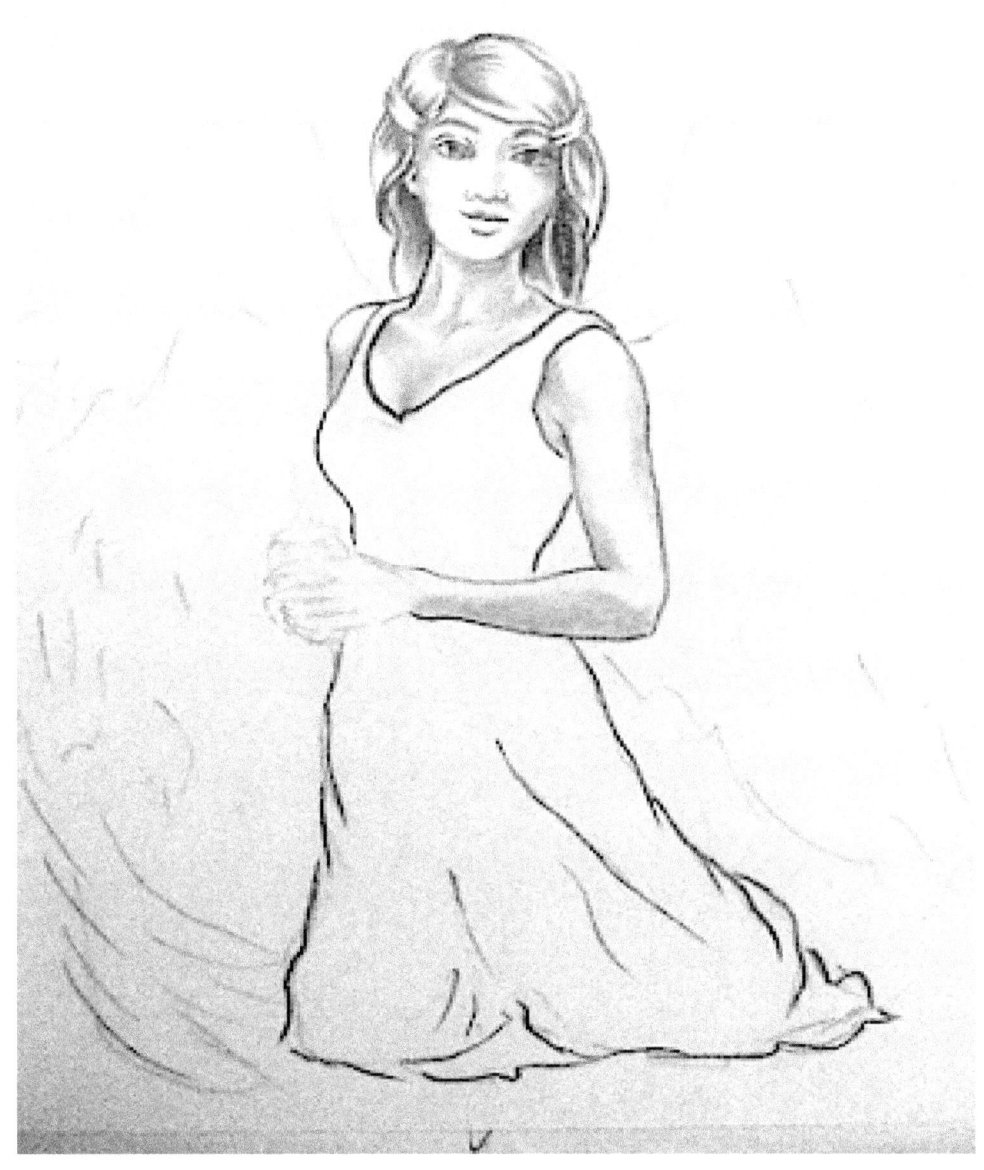

Add in the regions of shading shown in the drawing on her neck and arms.

Go over the outline and ruffles in the dress with darker marks.

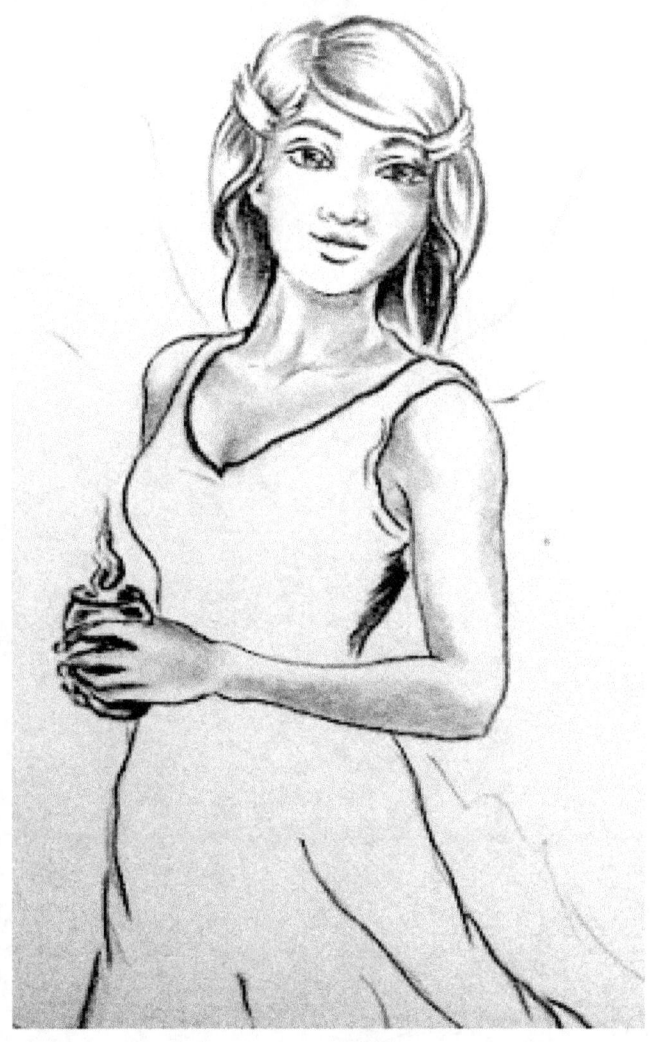

Add in the fingers and go over the can in her hands with darker marks and add small regions of dark shading to the can. Make a spiral shape above the can to suggest vapor rising from it. Add some shading to her left side underneath her underarm.

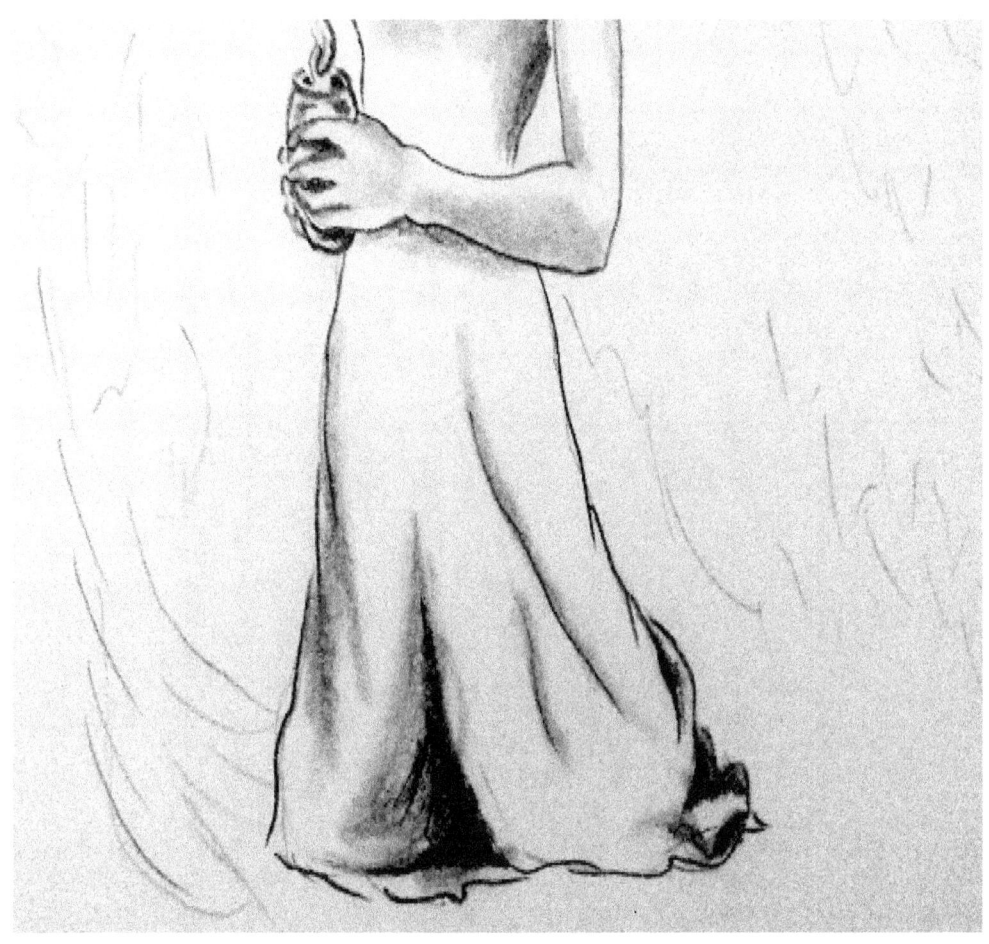

Do some subtle shading along the ruffles in the lower portion of the dress. Add some really dark areas of shading in the center of the lower part of the dress and the lower left.

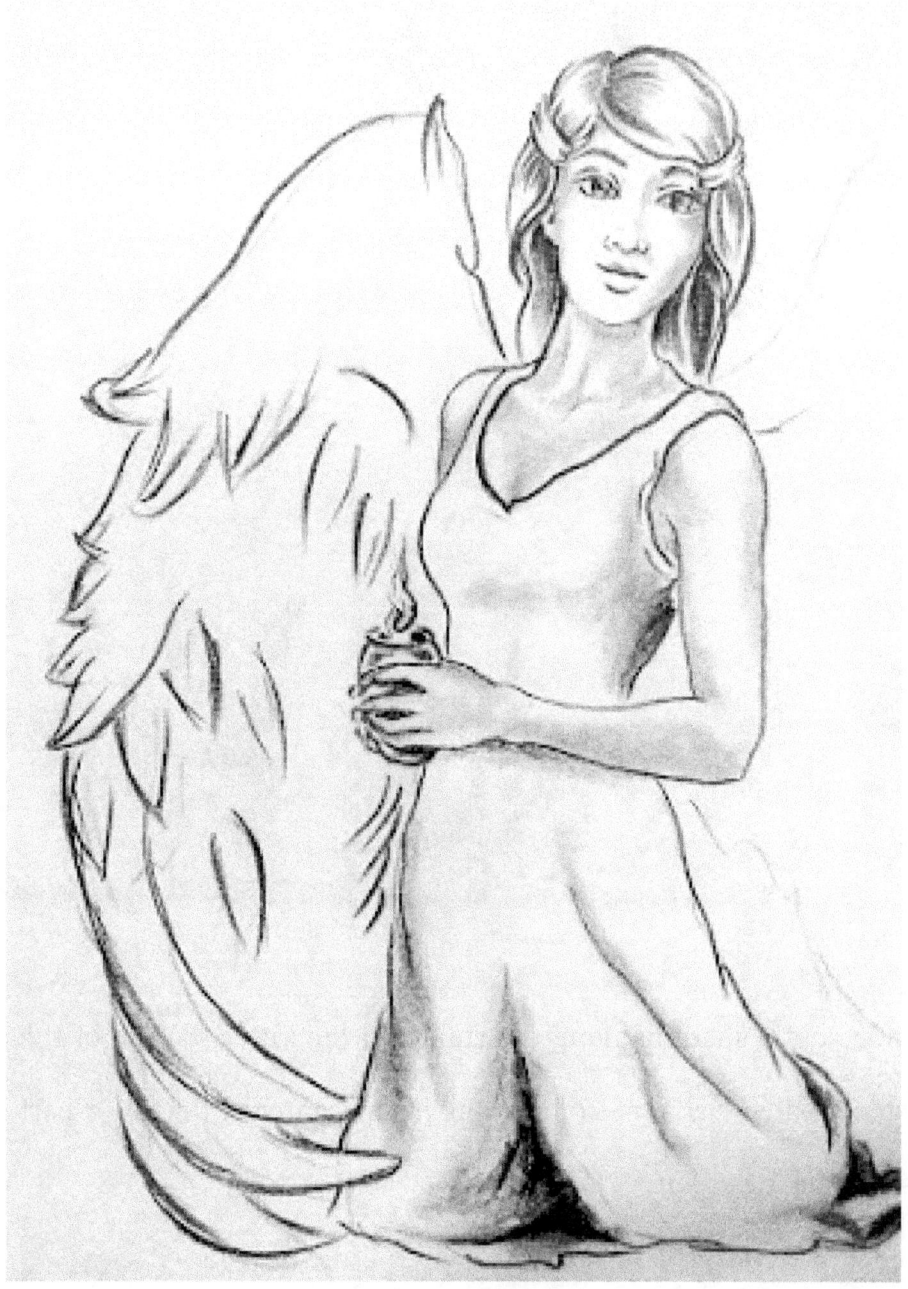

Go over the outline of the right wing. Add in the pointed shapes for feathers as shown in the drawing.

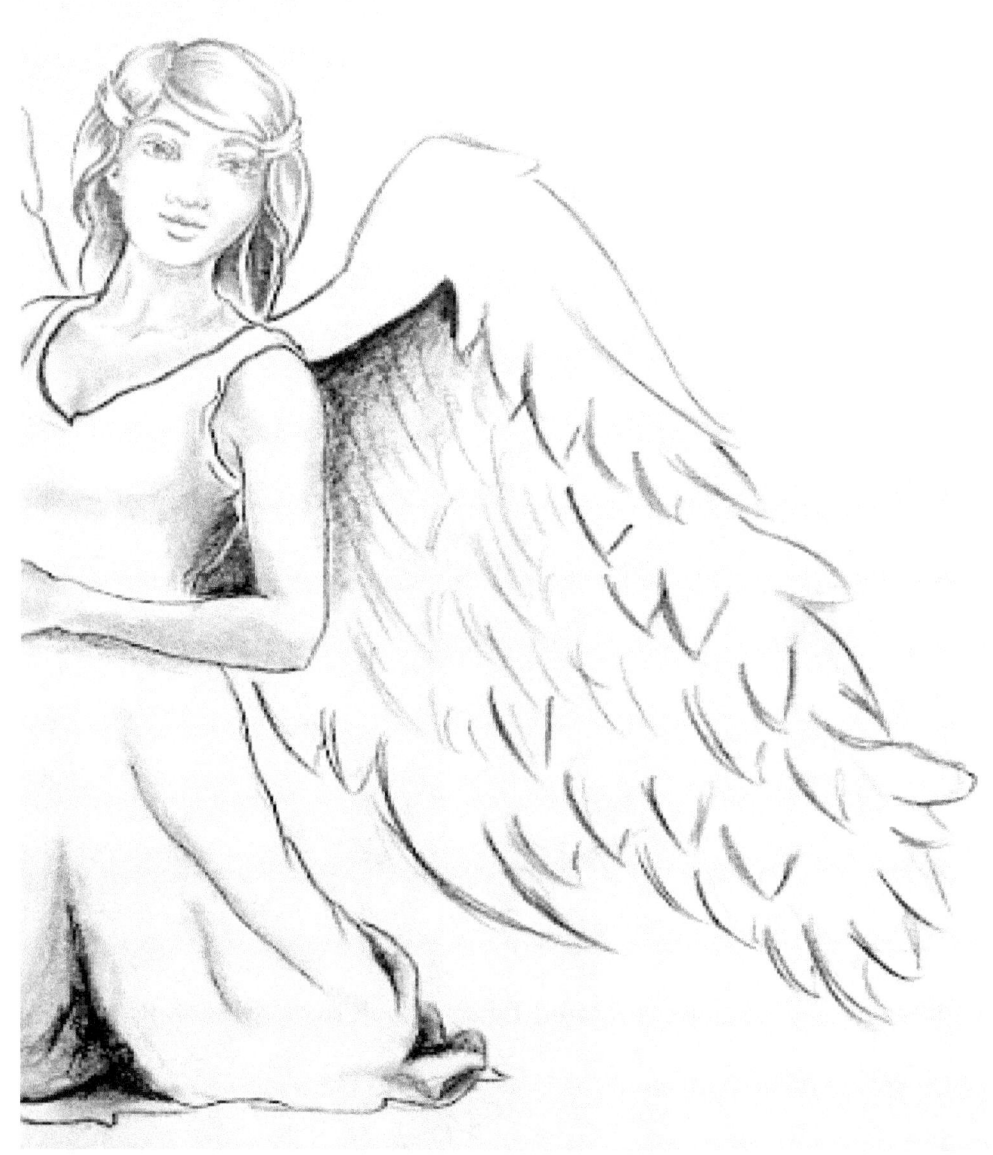

Now, go over the outline of the left wings with darker marks. Add several 'v' shapes to suggest feathers. Include some darker shading in the region where the arms meets the wings.

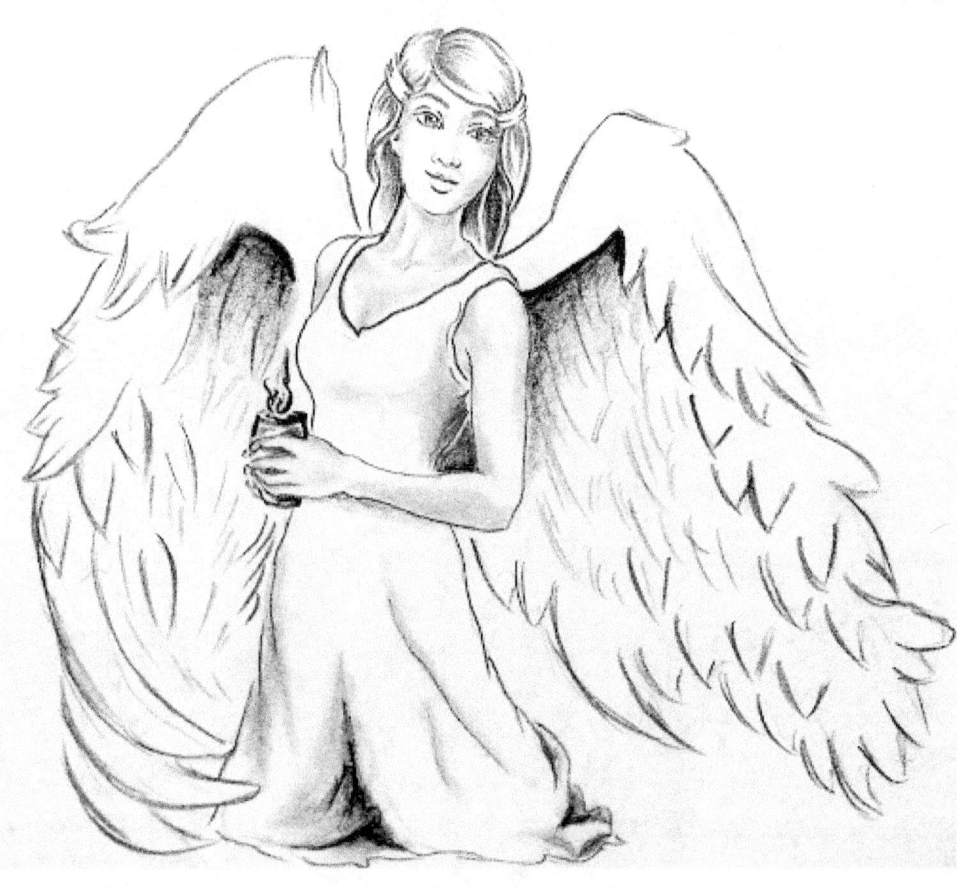

Now here's a look at the completed figure. Look over the details and fill in any that you may have missed.

Chapter 6 – Cat Woman

Cat woman is beautiful; but she looks like she could be trouble. On the television series, Batman, Cat Woman was a villain that would always be up to no good. This figure has her hand up like she might scratch you if you get too close!

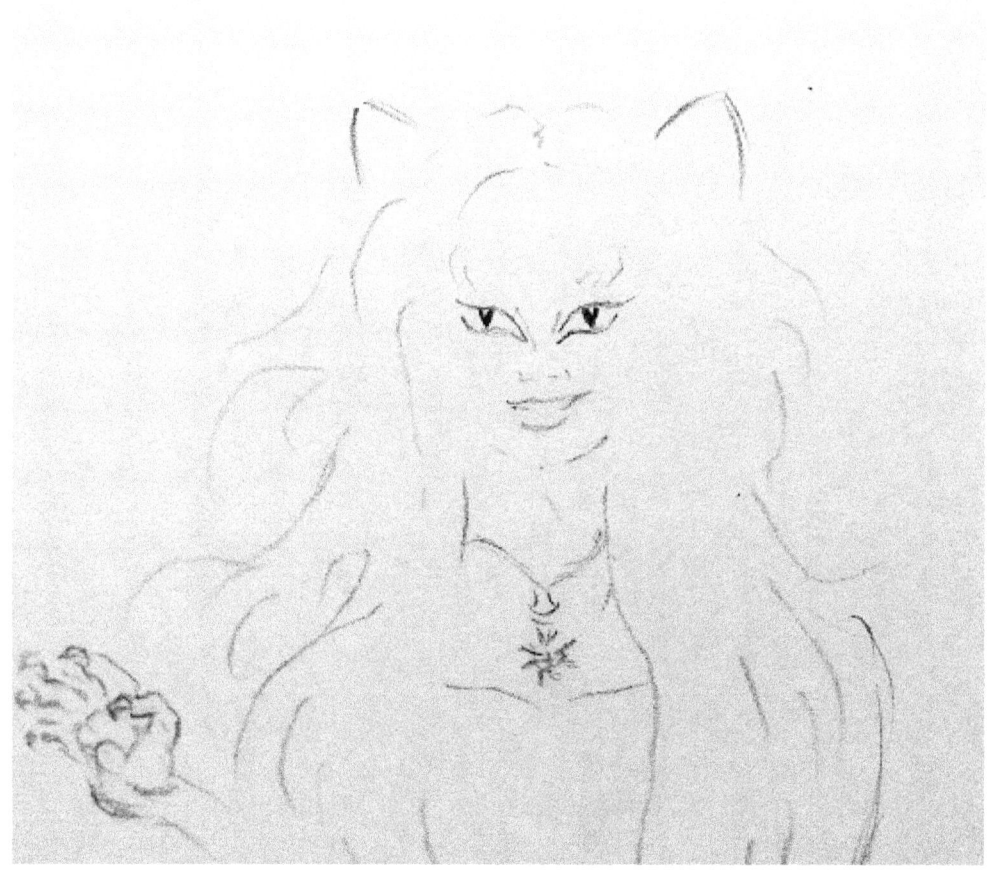

Make the outline of the figure using disconnected curved lines. Make two inverted 'v' shapes on either side of the head for ears. In the center of the head, make two pointed ovals that will be her eyes. Make two tiny 'v's inside of each eye to make the eyes look like a cat's. Draw in the nose and the curve of her upper and lower lips. Draw a skinny double line across her neck for a necklace and include a small star shape beneath it. On the right side, draw a clawed hand.

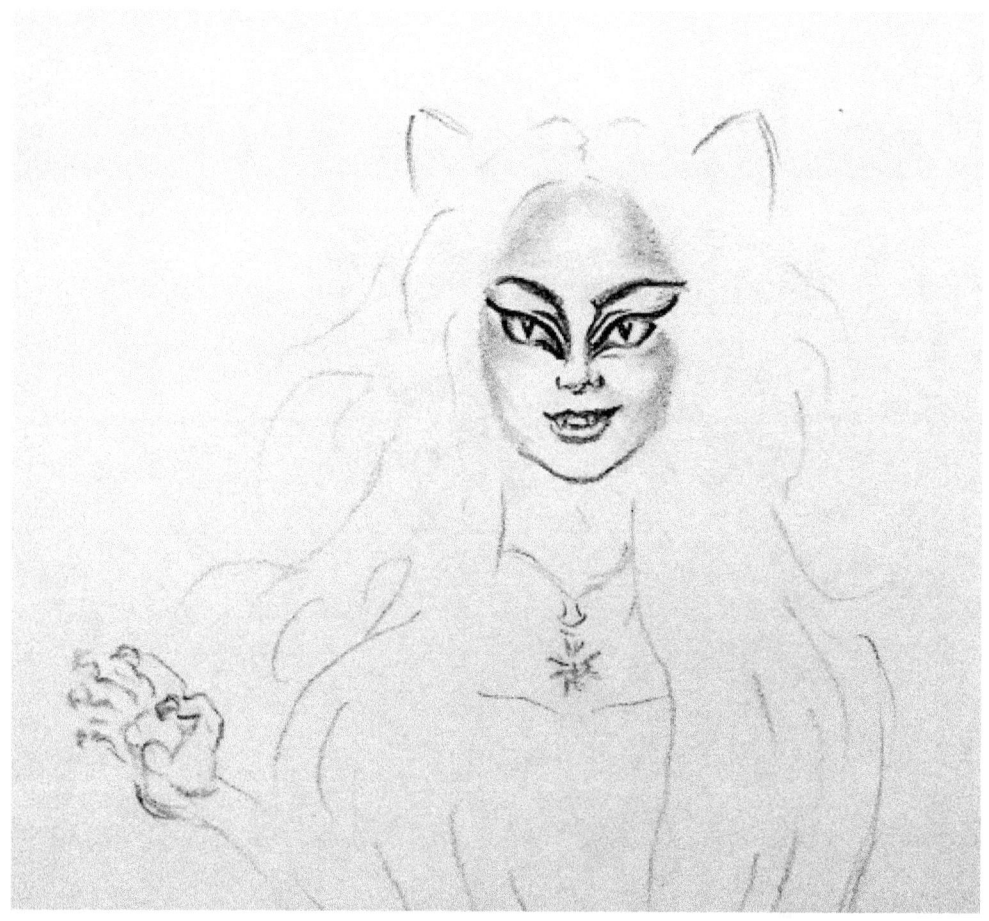

Do some light shading around the edges of the face. Draw two dark eyebrows extending down the bridge of the nose. Go over the outline of the eyes with dark marks. Add some fangs extending from the upper lip.

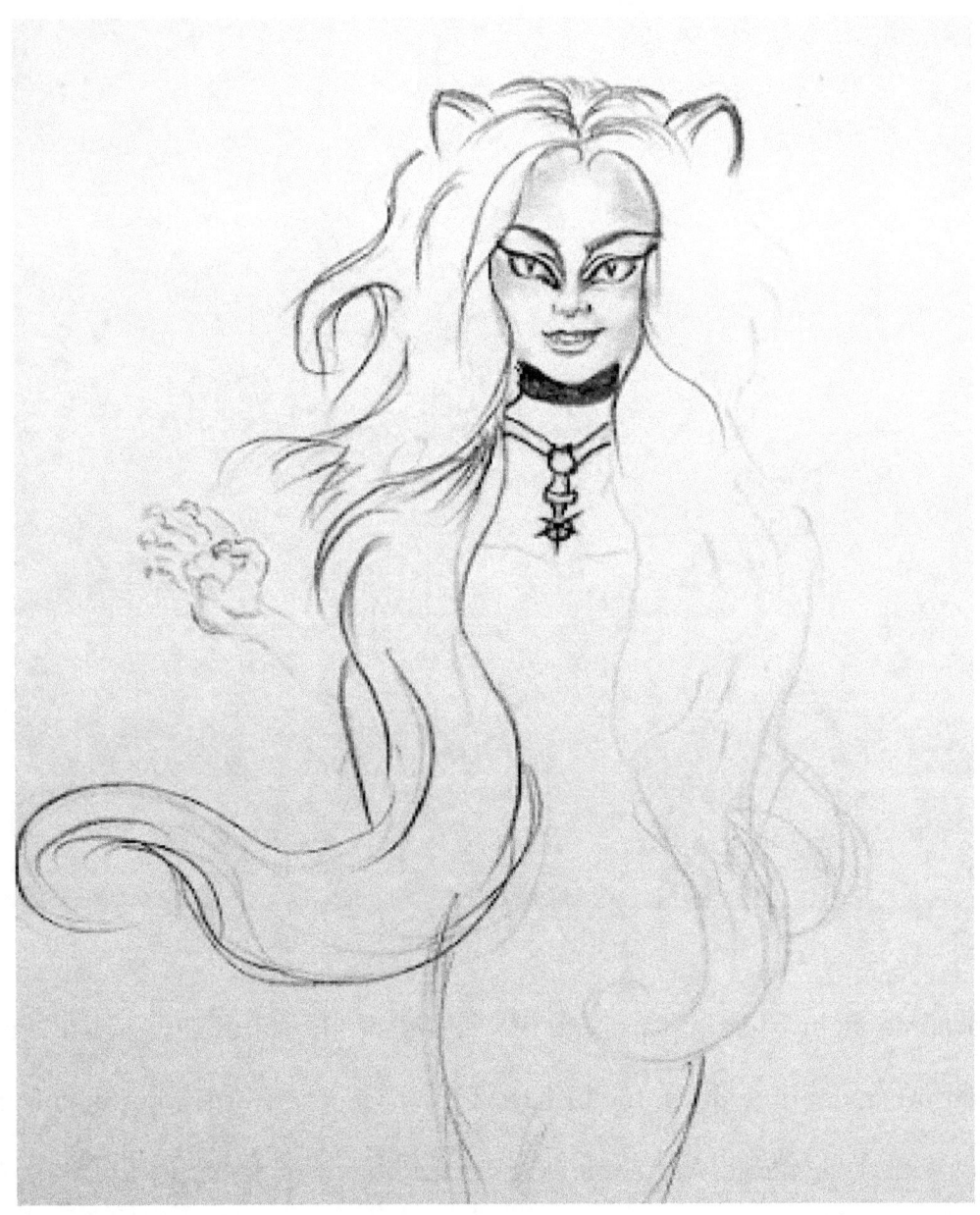

Draw the outline of the ears and several curved lines extending form the hairline (for hair). Make several long curved lines on the right that curls up at the end. Draw in a dark collar underneath her chin. Draw the necklace, making two bands that extend to a star-like amulet at the end.

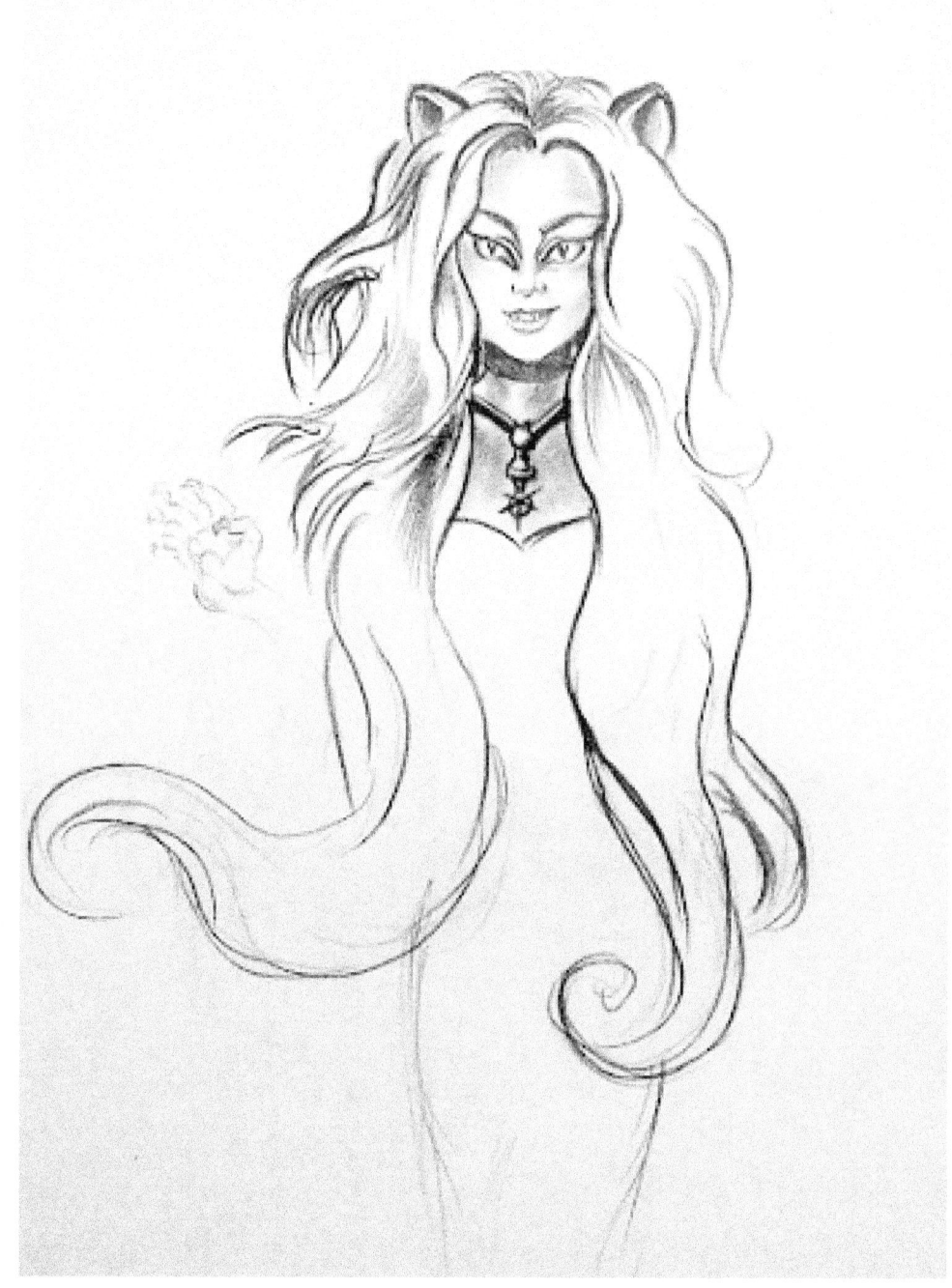

On the left side, add some long curved lines that curl up at the end to make

up her hair. Add some light shading to her chest and hair as indicated in the

picture.

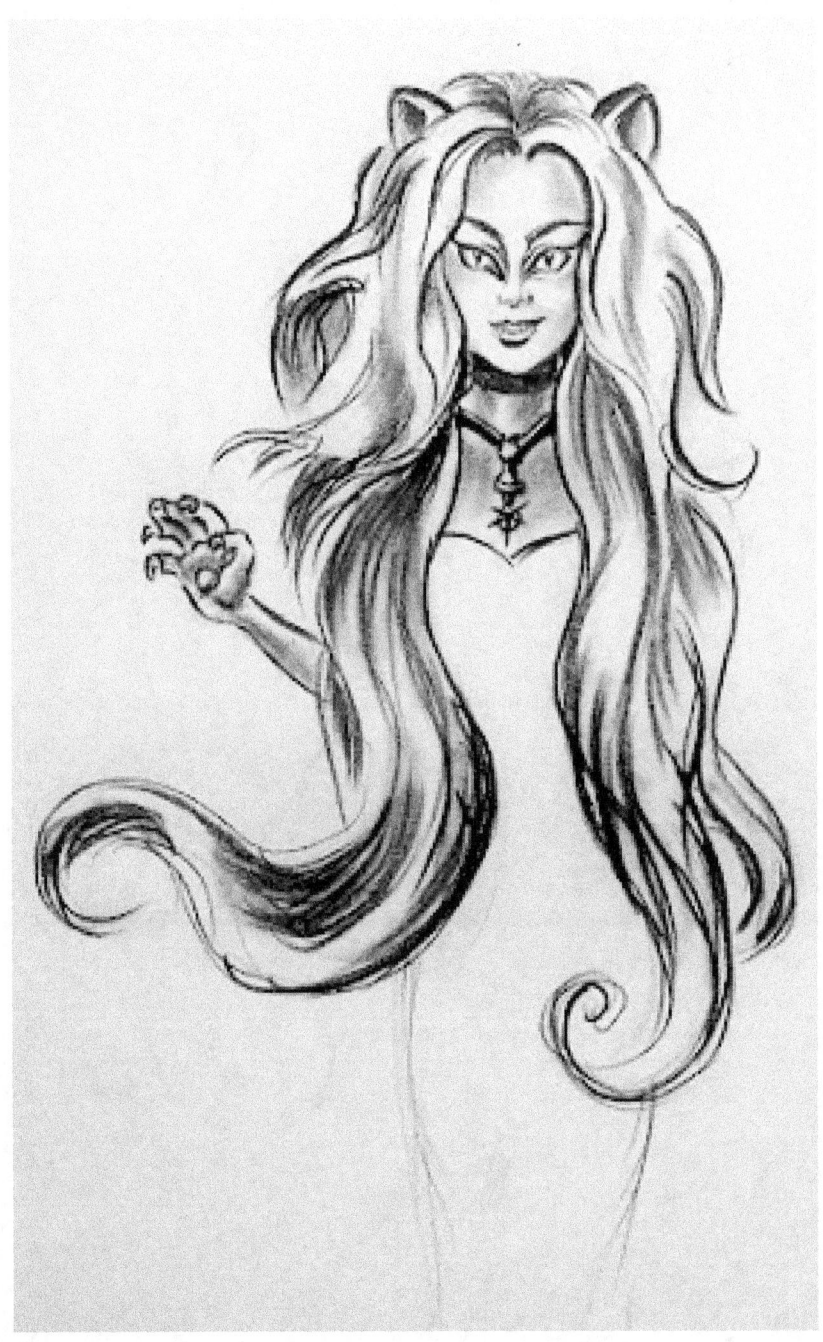

Go over the clawed hand and add some shading to it. Add the regions of darker shading in the hair as indicated by the drawing.

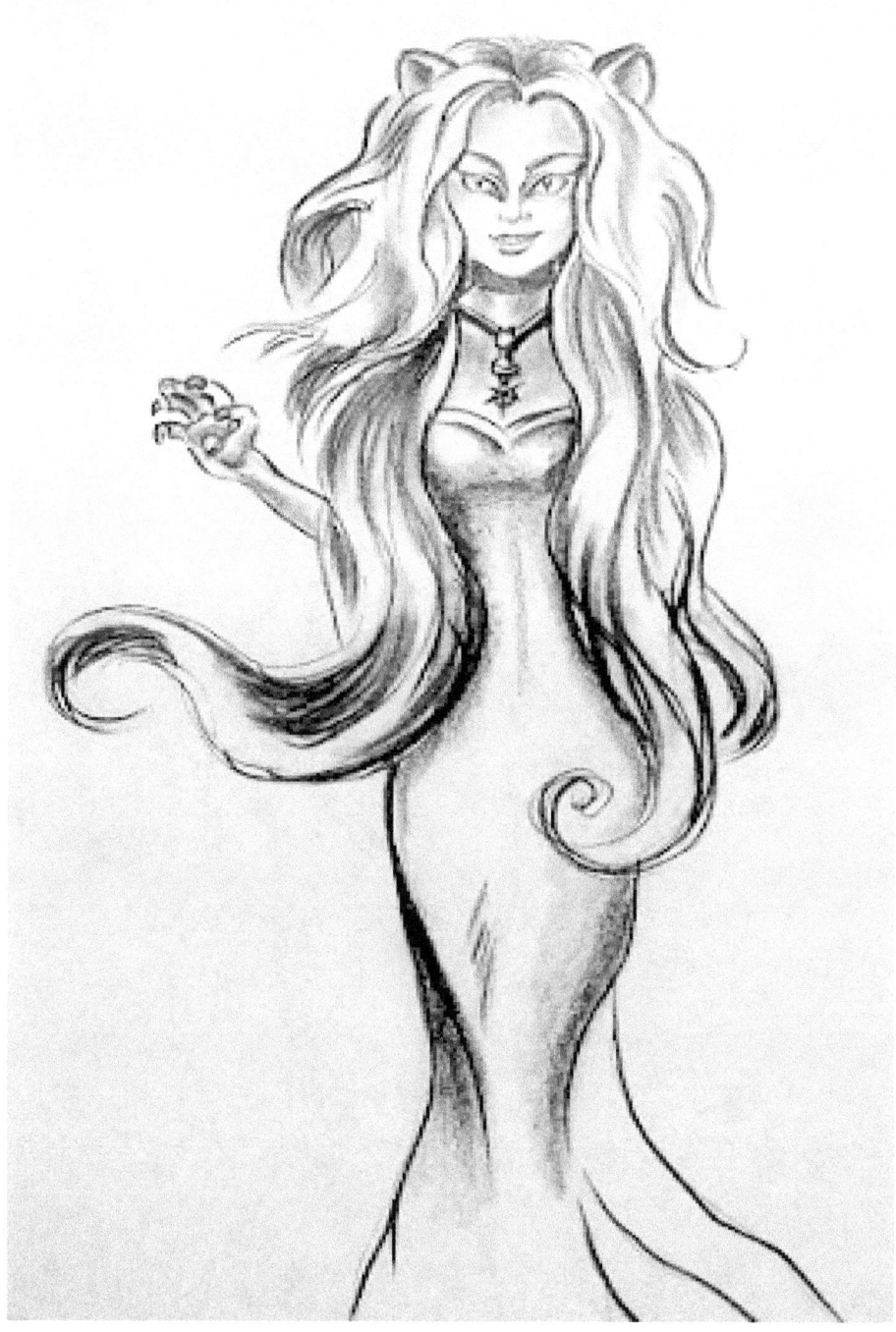

Add the stripe at the top of her gown. Add some shading to the edges of the

gown and go over the ruffles in the gown using dark, curved lines.

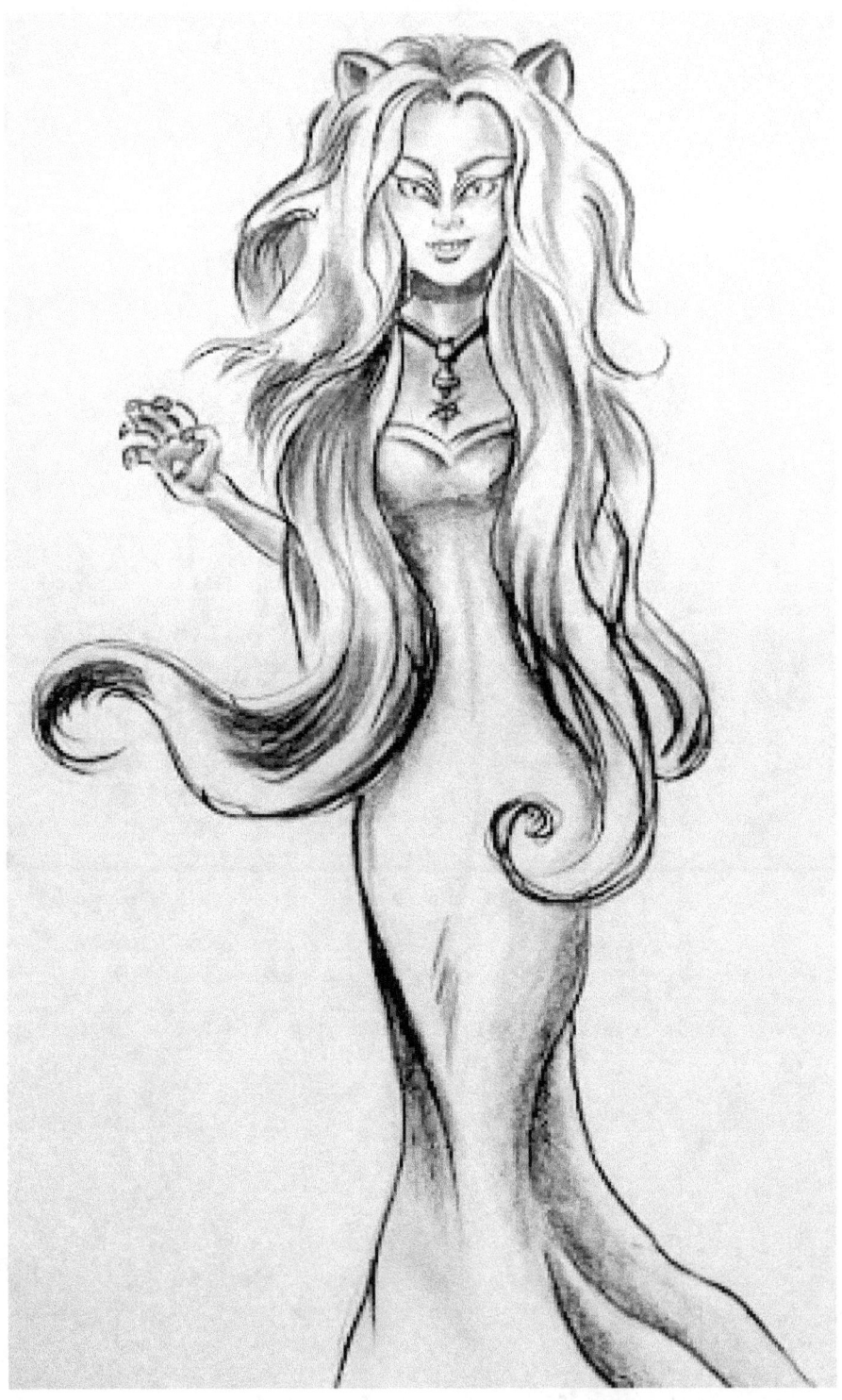

Add some more shading around the ruffles in the gown on the left side.

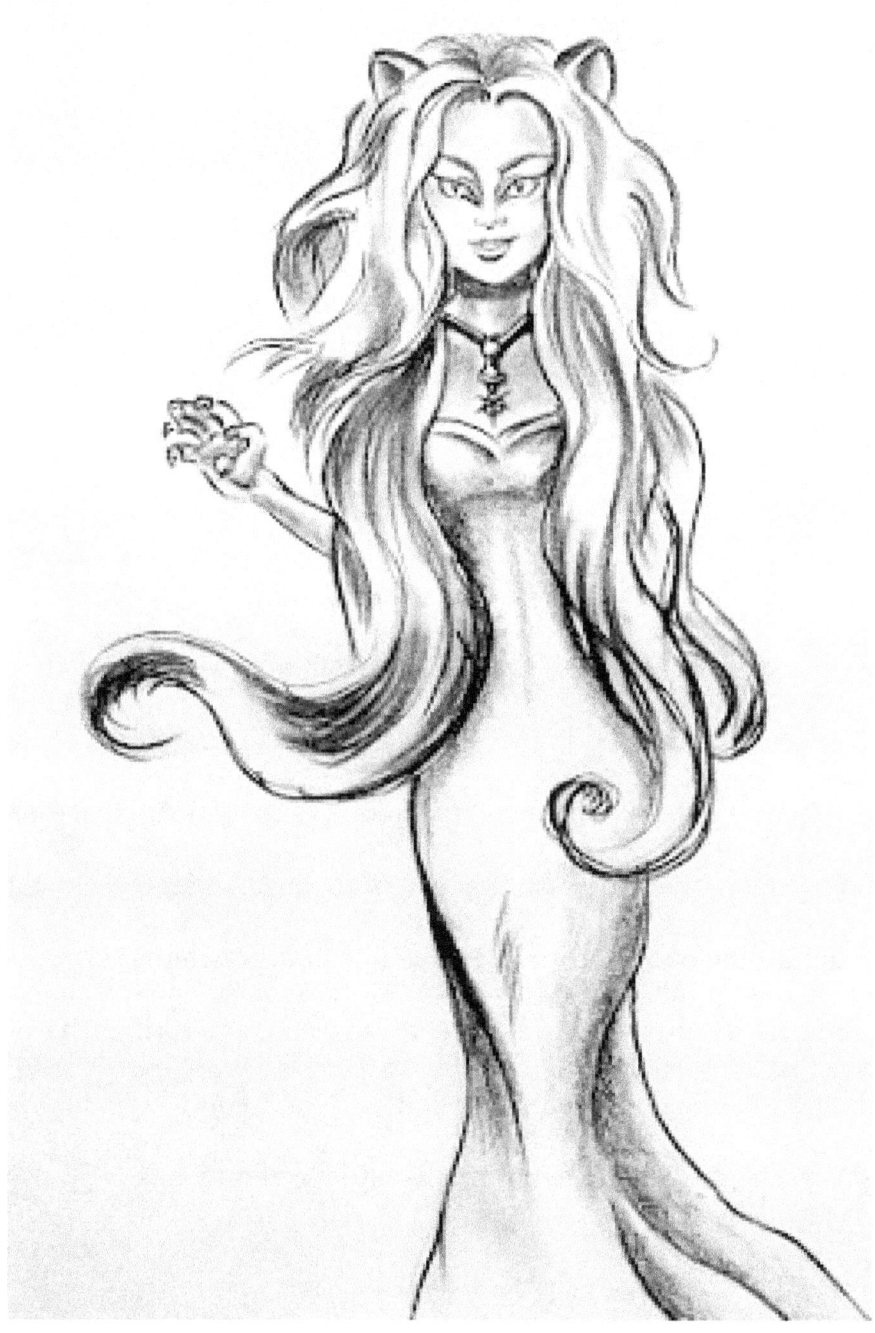

Here is the complete drawing of cat woman! Look and see if you left anything out and draw it in.

Conclusion

These mythological creatures will continue to capture our imagination; and for some people, they may even play a role in our faith. Fairies are very present in our fairy tales, movies and popular works of literature such as Peter Pan. Angels will continue to have a religious context, where they are thought of as guardians and messengers between heaven and Earth.

We hope that you have increased your ability to draw the female figure. The techniques used in this book should help you, in particular, with drawing facial features. The 'cross' technique helps you to space out eyes, nose and mouth correctly, a skill that can often be challenging. Once you use the horizontal line of the cross as the center point of the eyes, you erase it and have facial features that are correctly spaced. In addition, there is a lot of shading and stenciling technique that will help you to create a sense of contrast, which adds an element of realism to your drawings.

We challenge you to create your own fantasy girls, whether they be angels, fairies, elves, part human, part animal. We challenge you to make them come to life by depicting them in action, pouring potions or flying through the air. In this way, your creations can take on a life all their own. For example, you might create a girl that is part dragon or part dog. Either way we hope that we have helped to spark you imagination and have helped to sharpen your technique as an artist.

Other book by Long Mac

Dragons Drawing: Step by Step Guide (Fantasy Art Drawing Course Book 1)

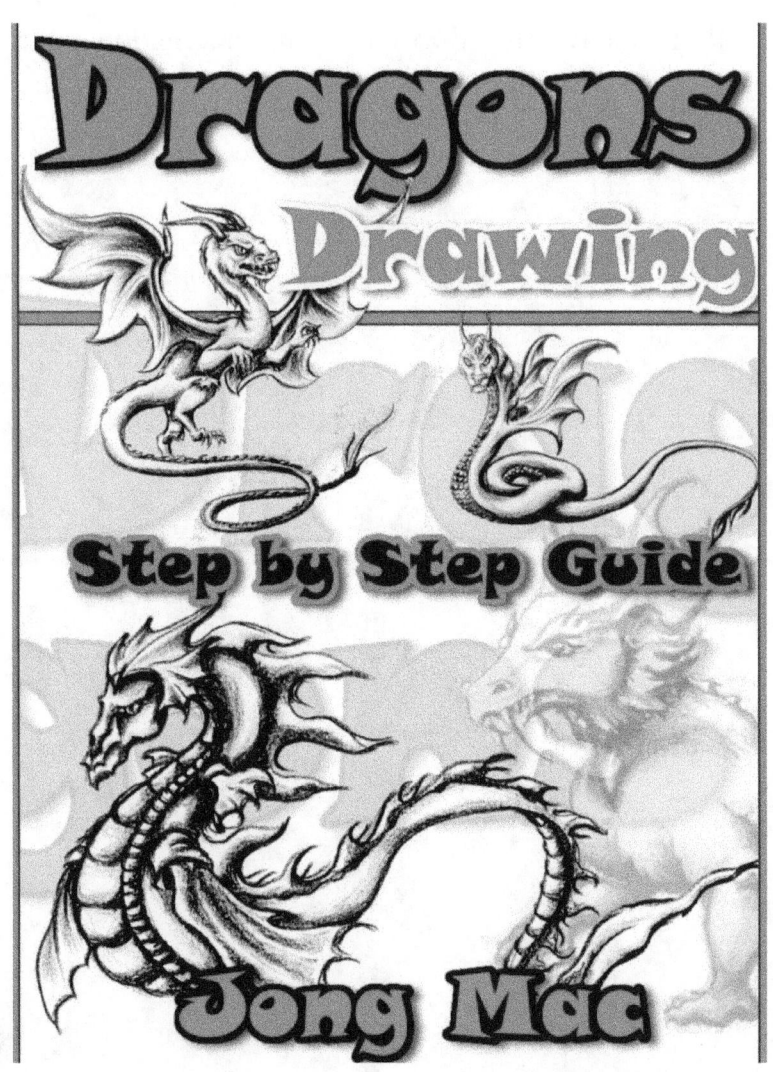

Thank you!

Thank you for choosing our book, we hope you found it interesting and helpful.

If you liked the book, please give us a favor to write your review.

We would really appreciate this!

If you would like to have a bonus – **FREE BOOK**, please send the screenshot of your review to this e-mail: **kelly.artbooks@gmail.com** and we will send you a **FREE BOOK** in PDF as a **GIFT!****

Hope to see you in our future books and good luck in your drawing experience!

** in the e-mail subject please mention the name of the book you reviewed and the author.

9 781532 867217